TDOD:

THE

DOMAIN

OF

DOTS

———————————————————————————

The Solitaire Art Game Created by Andrew DeGeorge

ISBN: 0692785906
ISBN 13: 9780692785904

How to Use This Book

A solitaire game is one you play against yourself. You play *The Domain of Dots* by picturing a dot-art design in your mind and then putting that design on paper using permanent markers. The first step is to select a reference graph from the eighty-eight offered in this book. Next, create your design by drawing dots in and around the reference graph. Use the graph to control the exact placement of the dots. For example, a player might choose a reference-graph line to run a string of dots parallel to, or he or she might add an arrangement of dots around where two reference-graph lines intersect. Then check the back of the reference graph or presentation side to ensure all your dots have soaked through the paper equally. Most permanent markers will soak through the paper and leave just the dot-art image. It's a good idea to check that all your markers can do this before starting. Finally, review your design for any missing dots.

The challenge of the game comes from the reference graphs. While they come in a wide variety of designs, the majority of them have some form of symmetry. Players can choose to take advantage of this symmetry or not as they create their dot art (a.k.a. TDOD). The truth is this: reference graphs both help and hurt your chances of making a winning design. Some graphs have been designed to assist you in creating simple TDODs. The challenge with these is to make something more interesting than what the reference graphs are persuading you to create. Then there are other reference graphs on which you might struggle to create any sort of design!

Here's what you will need to do to create a winning design. One, you have to "hold symmetry." This means controlling where subgroups of dots go on the reference graph. Two, you have to "maintain pattern." This means your design shouldn't have any extra or missing dots. Three, you have to ensure the dots are all of the correct size and color. It's also really important that all the dots are as round as you can make them. They shouldn't be too light or dark either. Follow these rules, and you will be on your way to a great TDOD.

The TDODs you see on the front and back covers can be grouped into two general types. One is a "full-field form," where you fill up a space with dots that use color, size, and spacing to form a design. The other type is a "complex chain." Here you use a repeated sequence of dots to form a chain that makes an interesting shape, or the chain as a whole creates some form of symmetry.

So, how do you win this game? Well, it's a solitaire art game, and it can be said that art is in the eye of the beholder. Therefore, it's really up to you if you think you've won. Here are a few ways you can judge yourself or have somebody else judge your TDOD, though. The front cover of this book shows some TDODs I feel were winning efforts. The back cover shows some failing efforts.

1.   Did you "maintain pattern" and "hold symmetry" throughout the entire game?

2.   Are the dots consistent in shape, size, and color?

3. Can other players guess which reference graph you used to make your TDOD? (If they can't, it shows you've been very creative.)

4. Finally—and most importantly—are you really happy with the way it came out?

I judge my TDOD by asking this question: Can I see myself wearing it on a T-shirt? UberPrints.com is a website that digitally prints you a single custom T-shirt. This can be done after you have scanned your TDOD into your computer to make a PDF. I have had UberPrints.com turn a few of my TDODs into T-shirts and found that the process of creating and ordering them was quicker, easier, and cheaper than imagined. One trick I missed while ordering a shirt was to add "print graphic at maximum size" in the notes section of the web page. Including this note produces the largest image of your TDOD onto the shirt.

Markers

Good permanent markers to start with are ArtMinds® dual-tip permanent markers, which can be found at Michaels® arts-and-crafts store. The ink in these markers soaks through the paper easily, leaving a clear dot on the back side of the page. Also, the second tip is convenient because it can make very small dots. I have found that professional-grade markers work as well. They are a lot more expensive, so maybe ask the store manager if you can check that the ink soaks through a standard piece of copy paper before buying.

Common Errors to Avoid

It's better to show than to tell, so on the back cover are examples where my TDODs went wrong. Match the numbers below to the numbers on the back cover.

1. The dots in the middle section were added in one direction like beads on a necklace, while the dots in the top and bottom sections were added one color at a time. This threw off the spacing, which hurt the design's symmetry.

2. In this complex chain, you can see where I didn't "hold symmetry."

3. I didn't "maintain pattern" on this part, because a few small blue dots are missing.

4. It's important to know just how large you can make a dot before it stops being round. That's what happened with this large gray dot.

5. Another problem is adding dots that don't make a clear image on the finished side.

6. The opposite problem is also an issue, where dots can have dark patches.

These errors can be avoided with practice, but the most important thing to be aware of is that making an error early in the game is better than later. Early errors can be fixed by changing your design on the fly, so it might be a good idea to slow down and double-check more often as the game goes on.

Before you start, read the following

1. It is acceptable for the book's owner to make copies of the reference graphs. You might want to make several attempts on each.

2. Don't forget to blot. Remember to put *two* pieces of scrap paper under your reference graphs before you start your game. Even if you have made copies of the reference graphs, you should still use a couple of sheets to protect whatever surface you are working on.

This page intentionally left blank

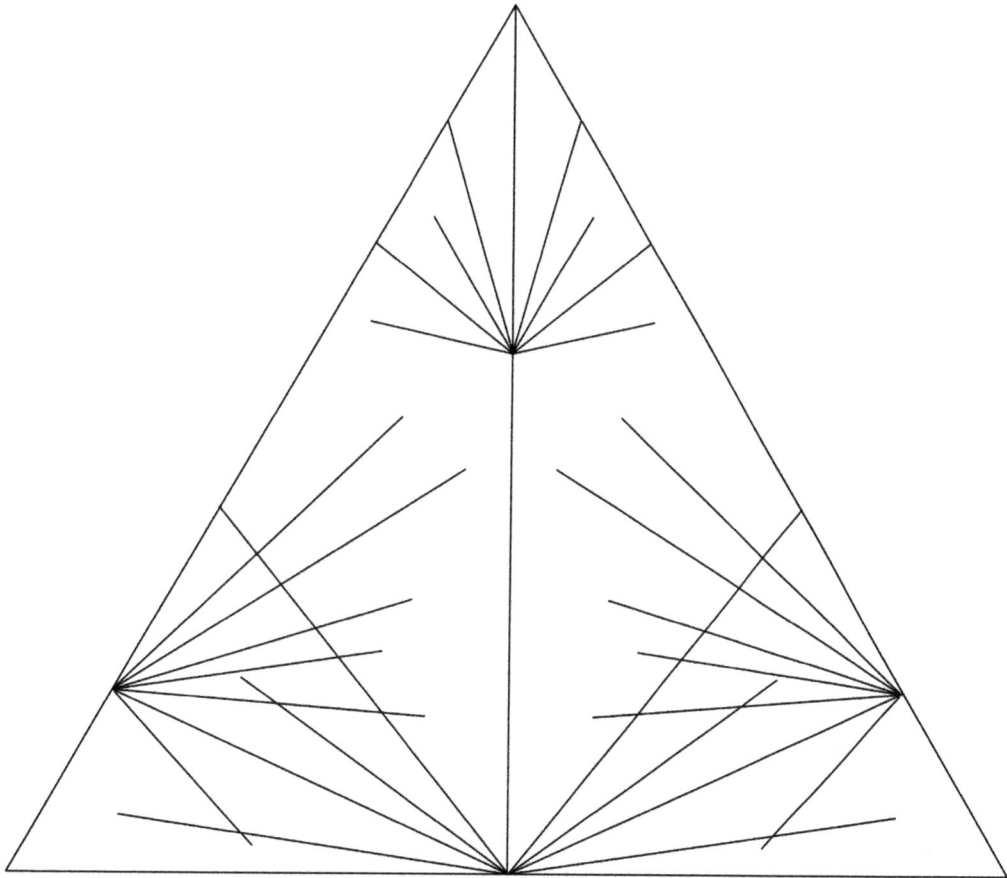

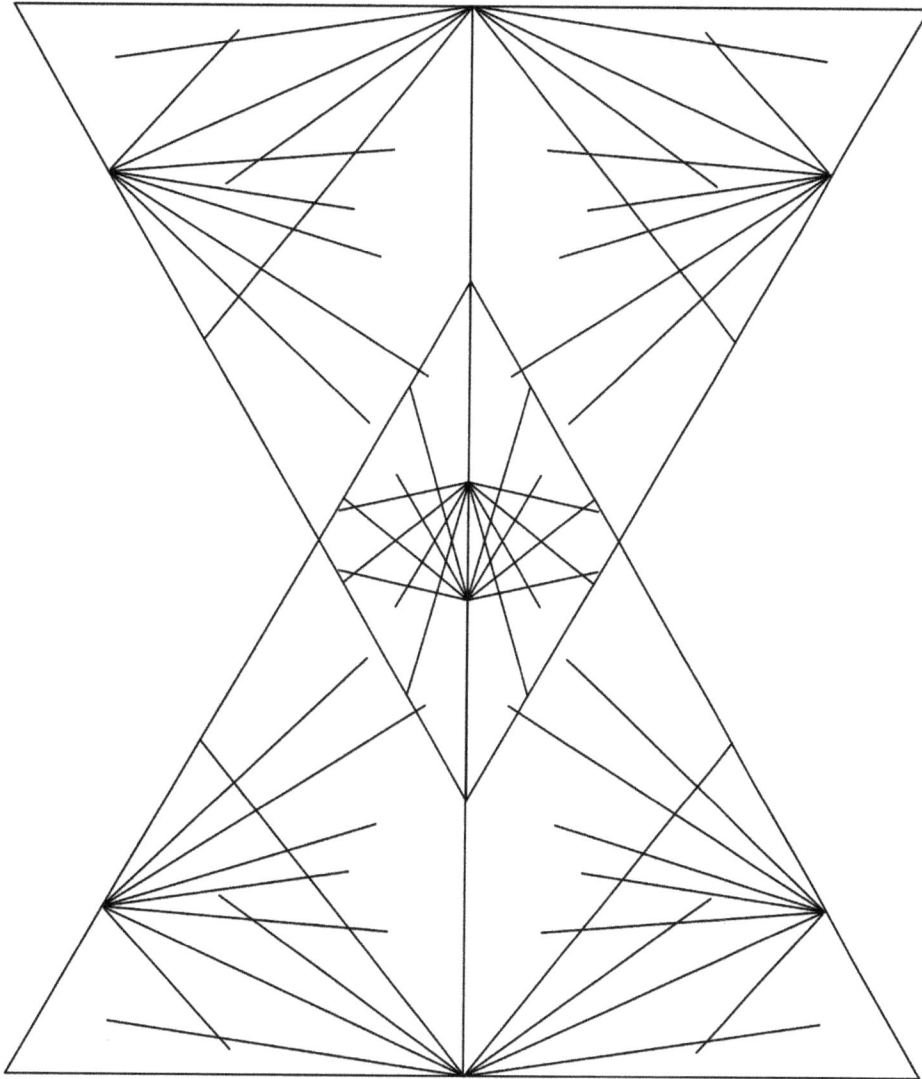

Reference Graph 2B

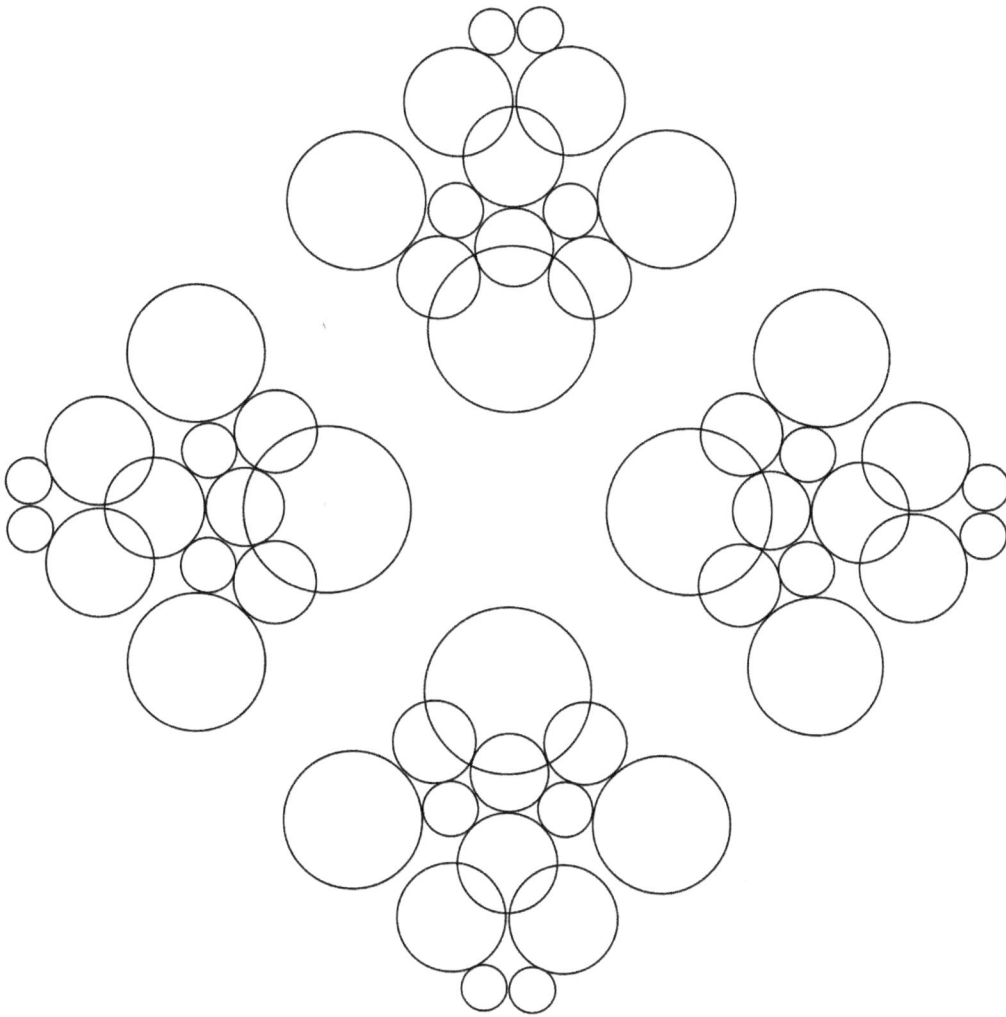

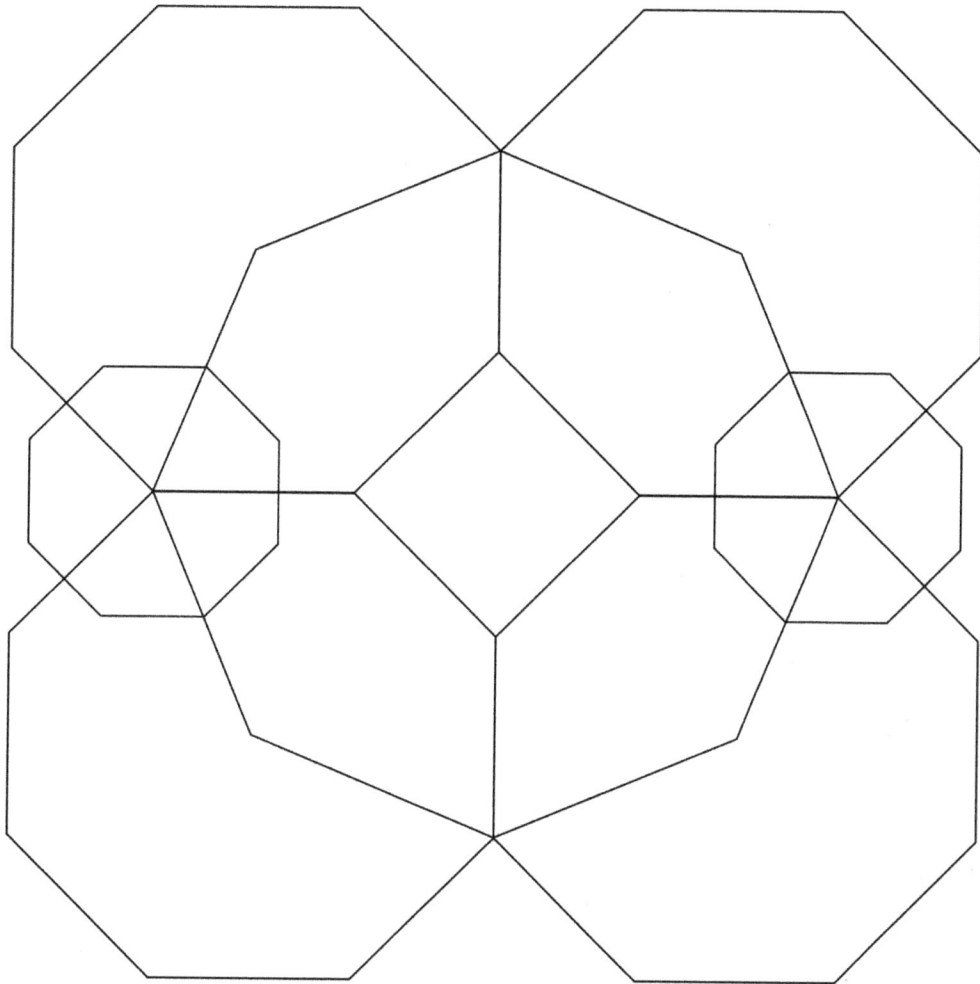

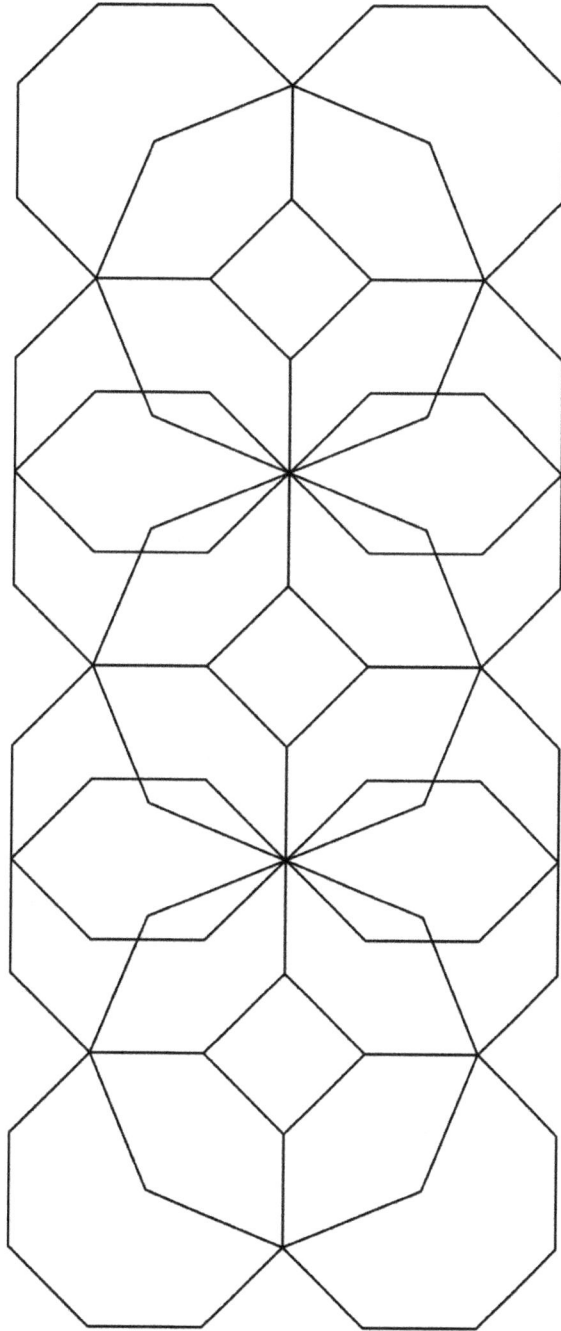

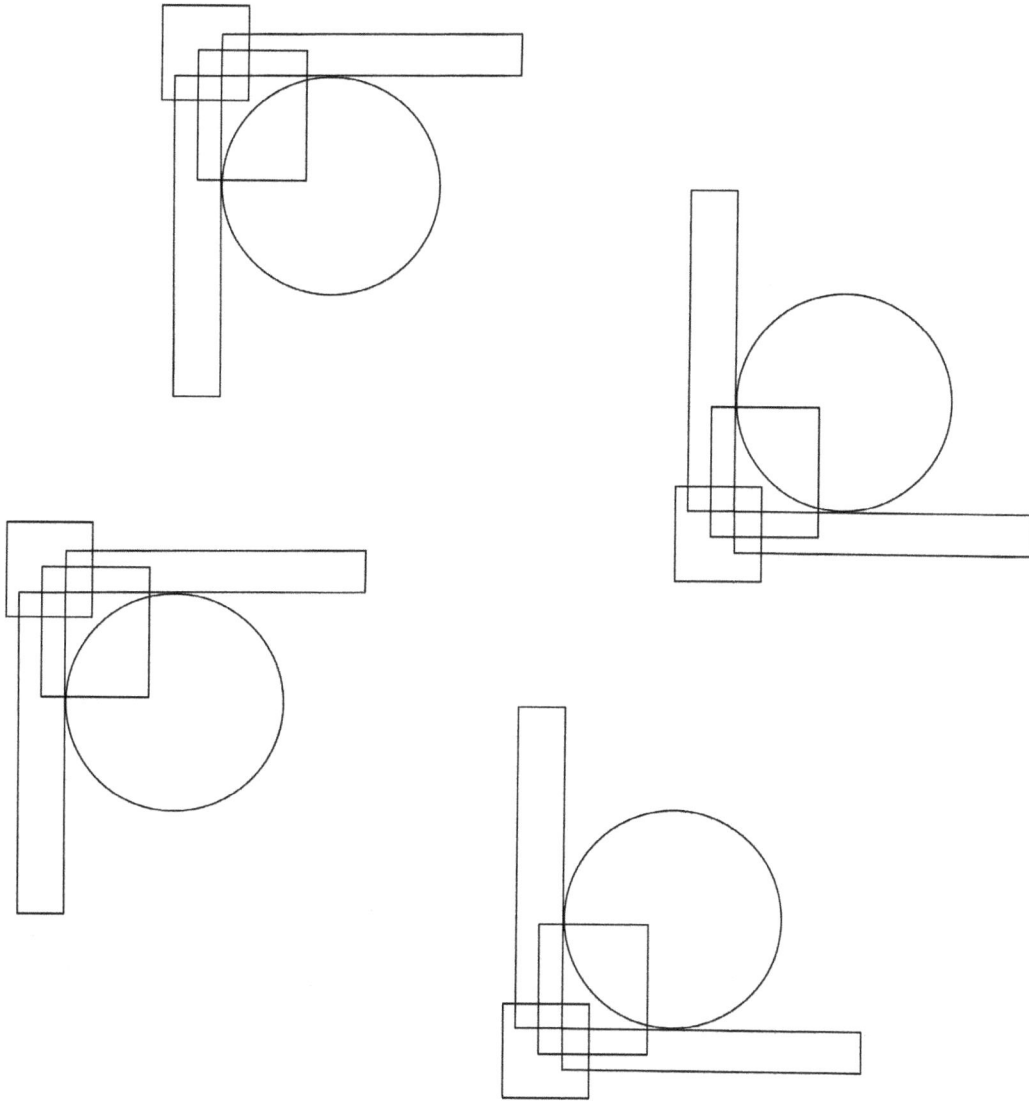

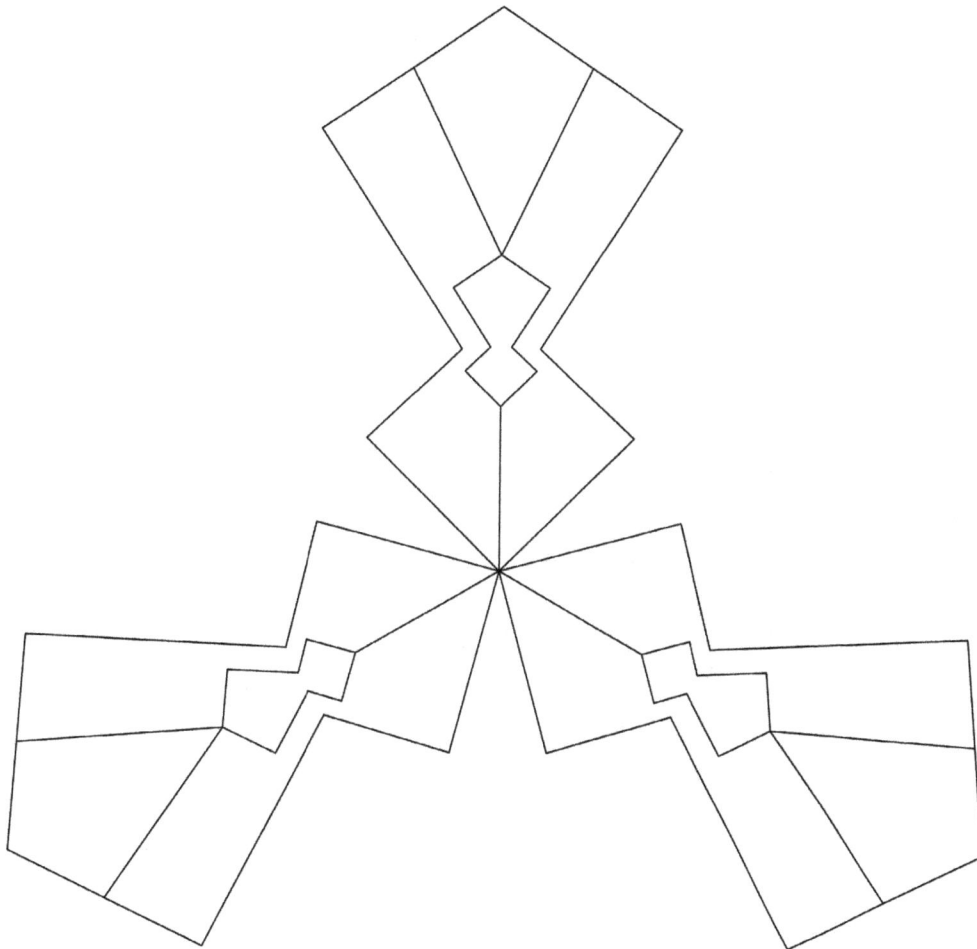

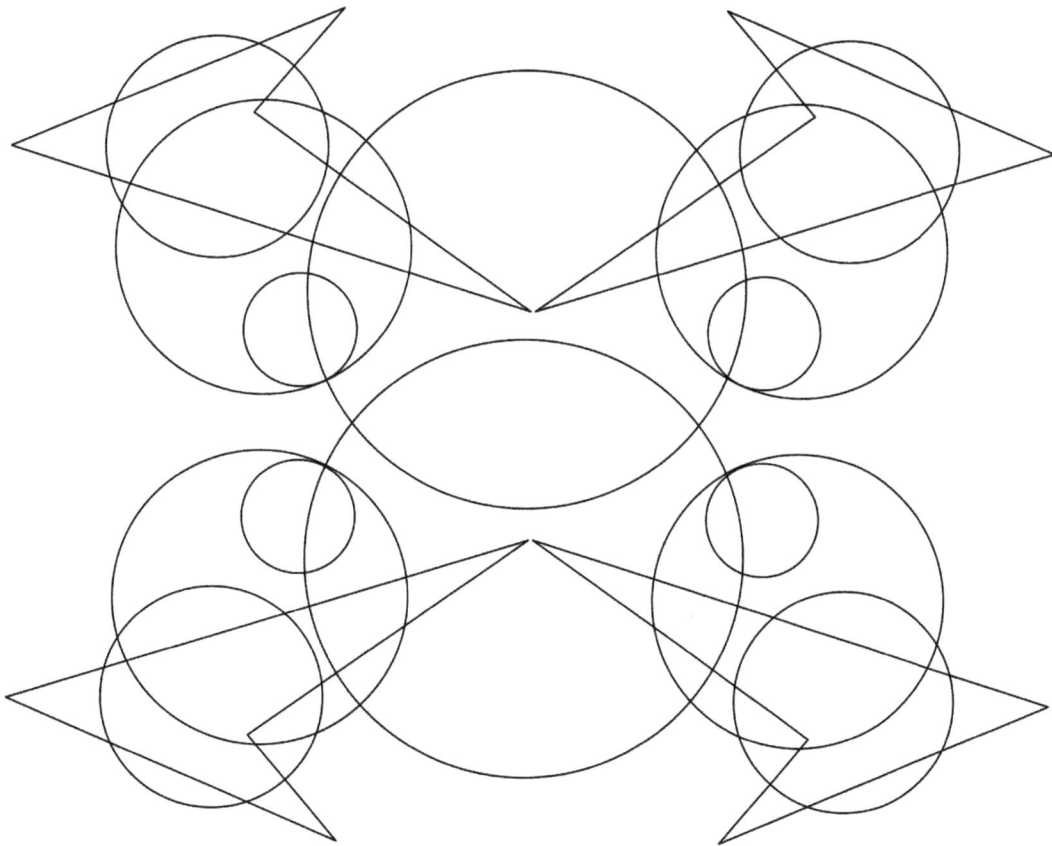

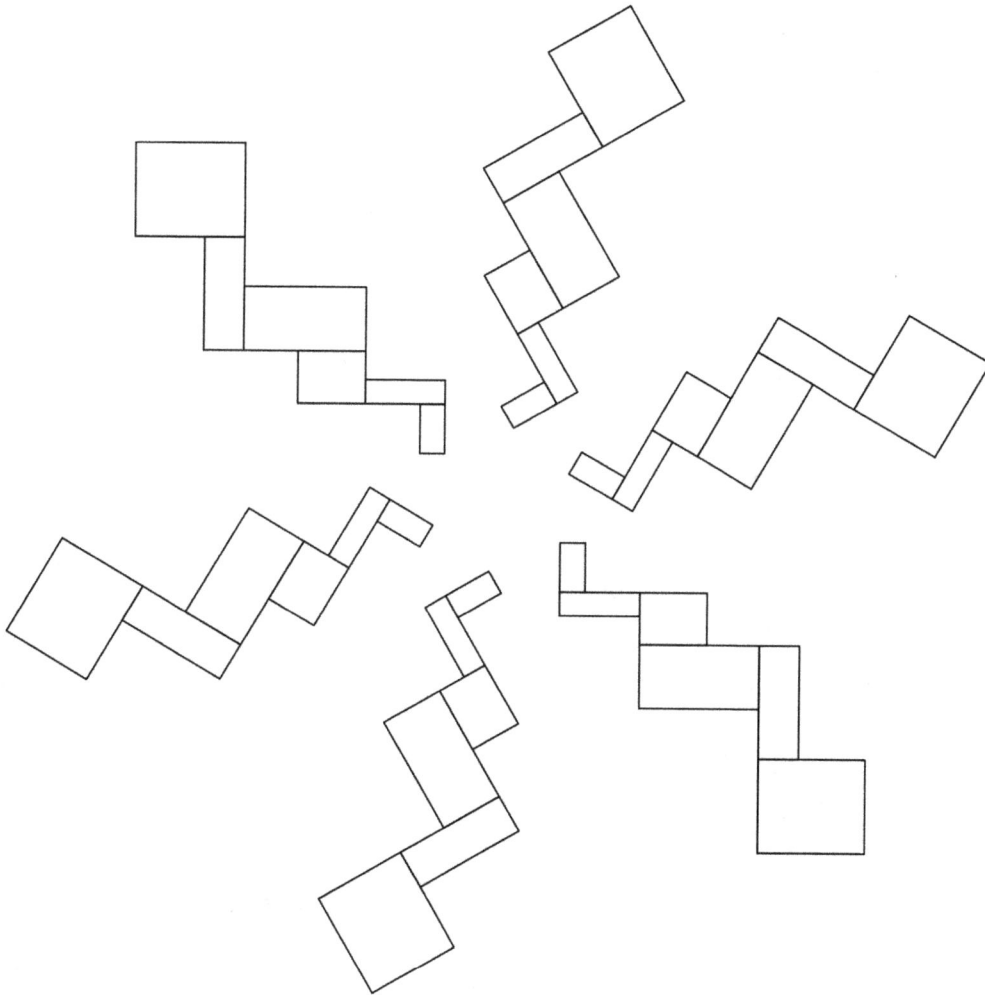

Reference Graph 7B

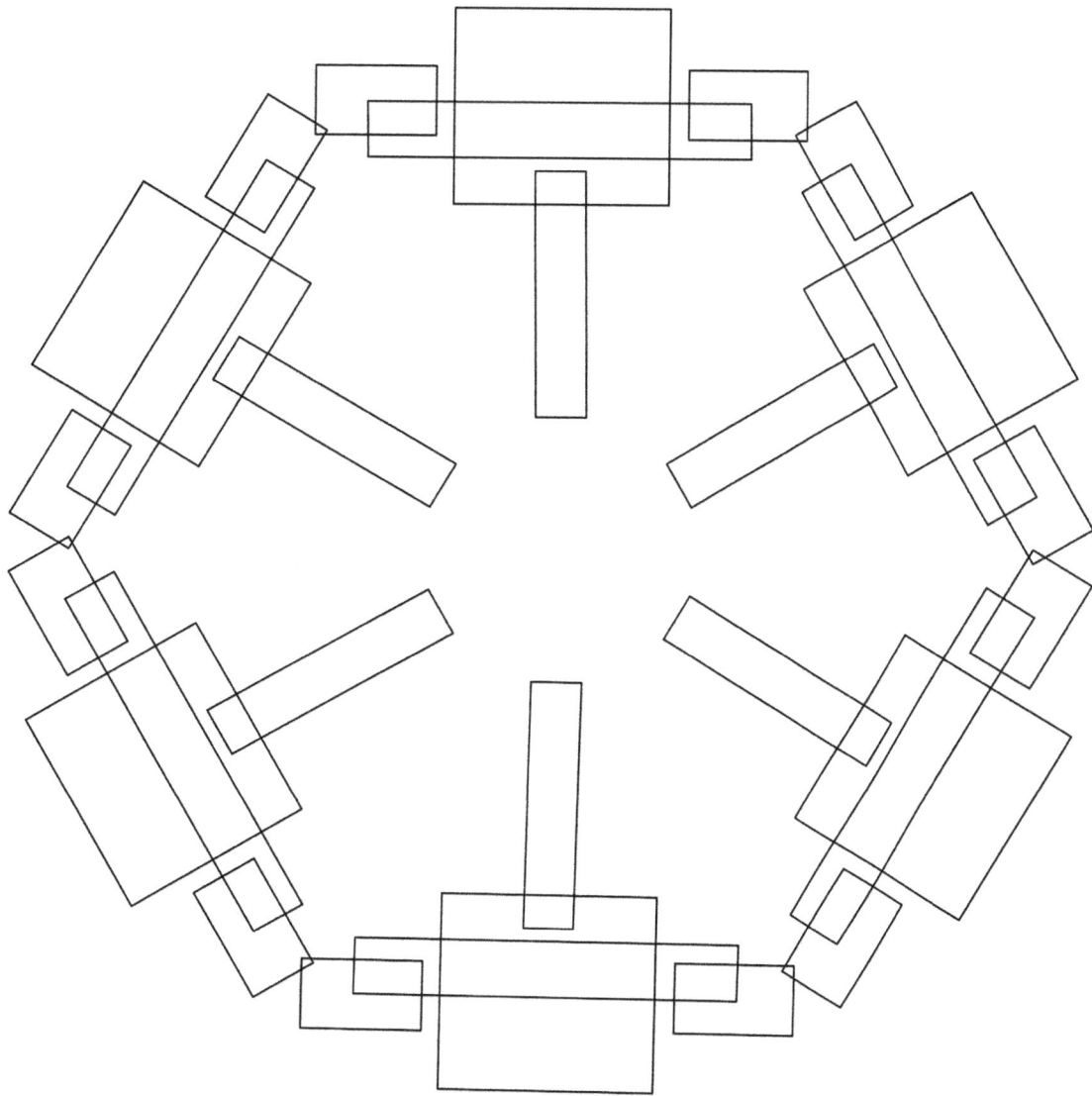

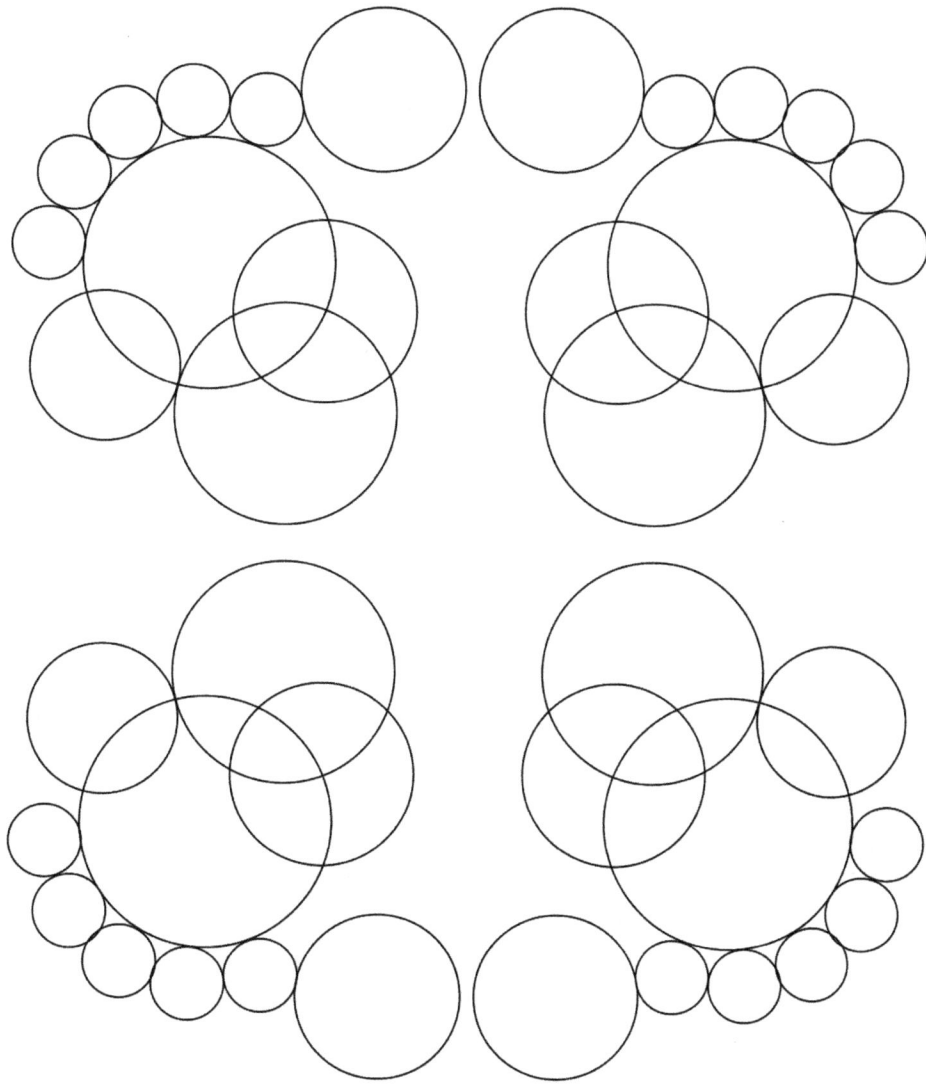

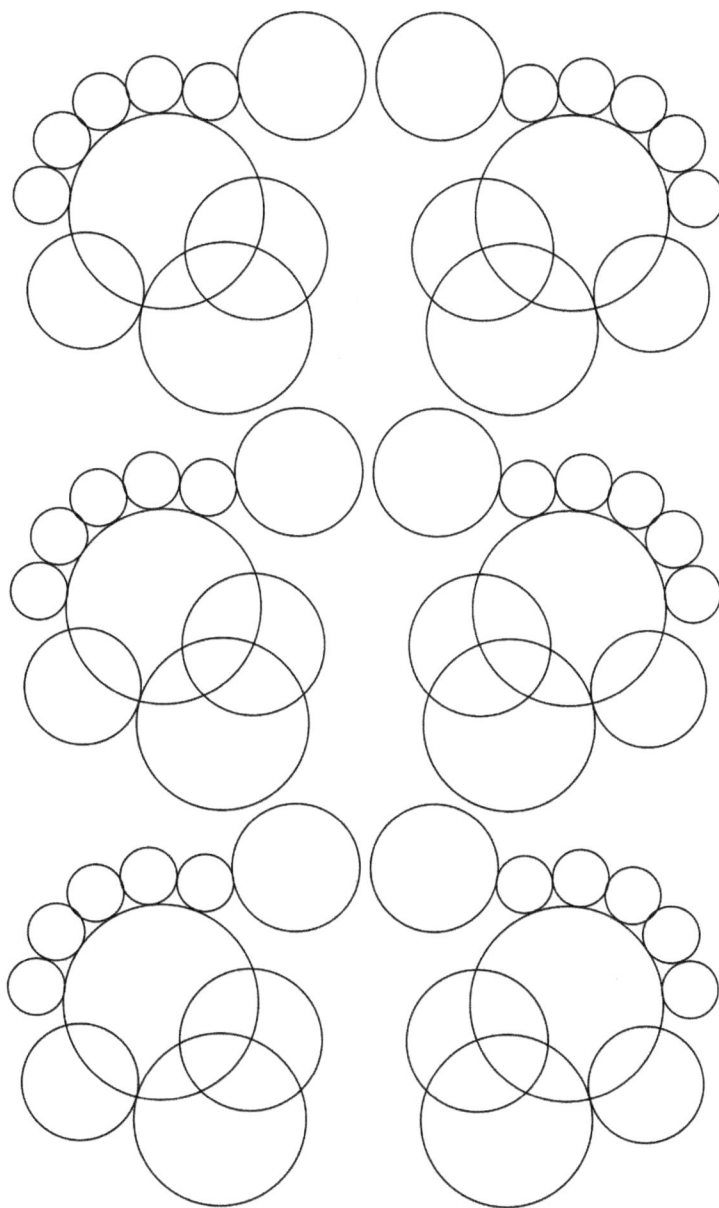

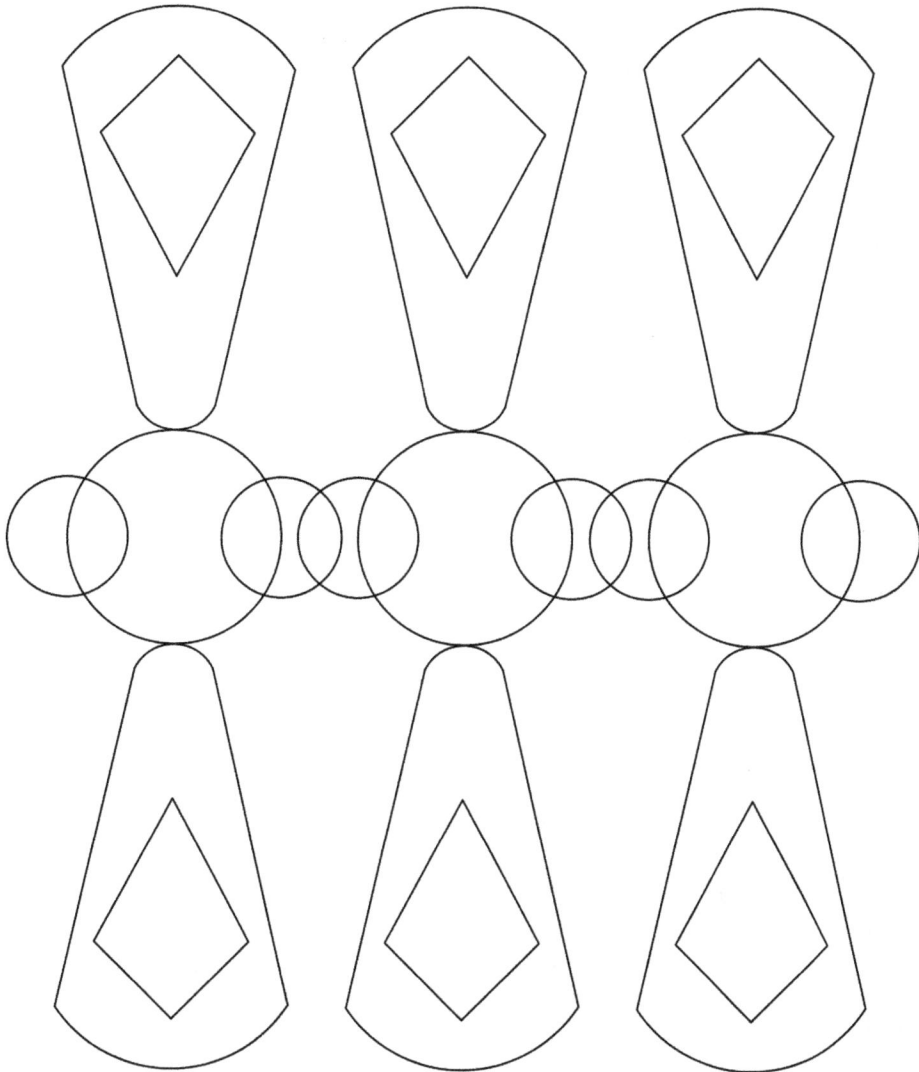

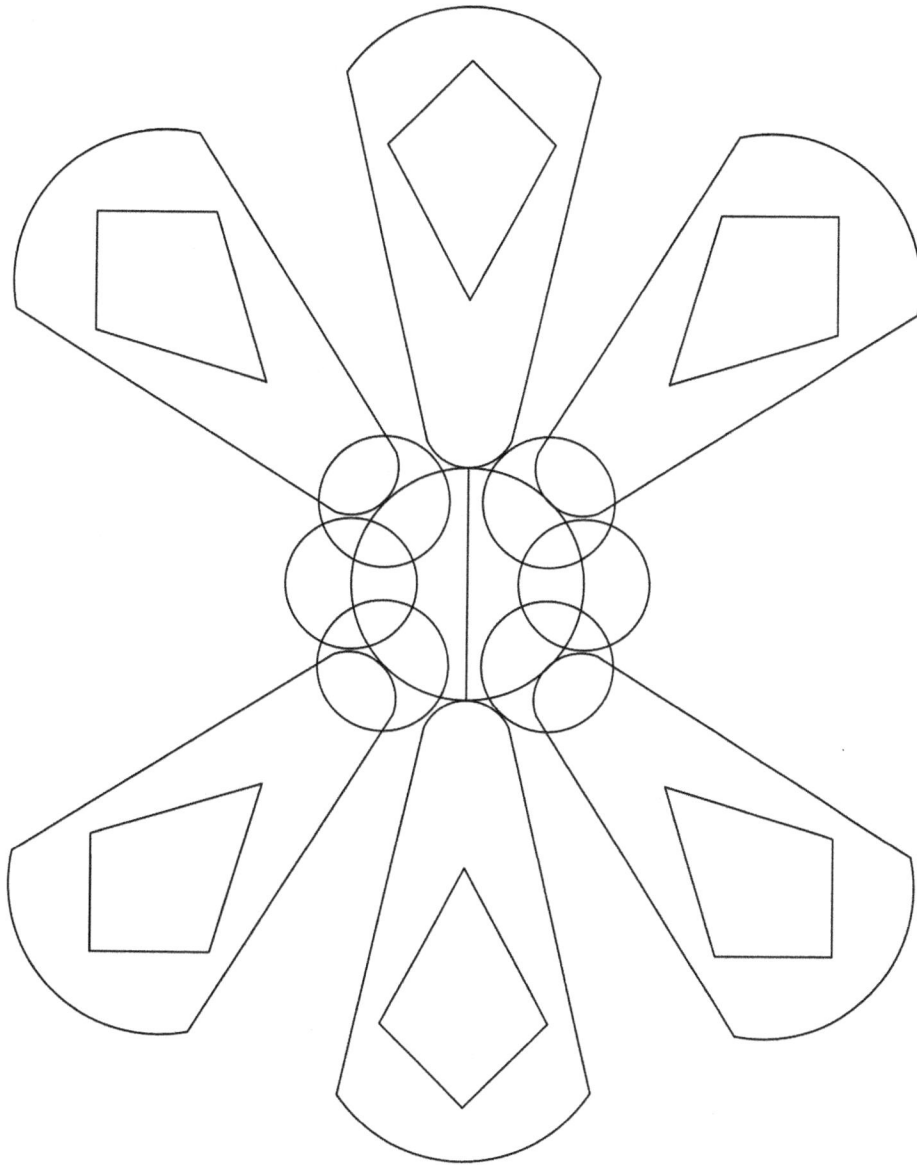

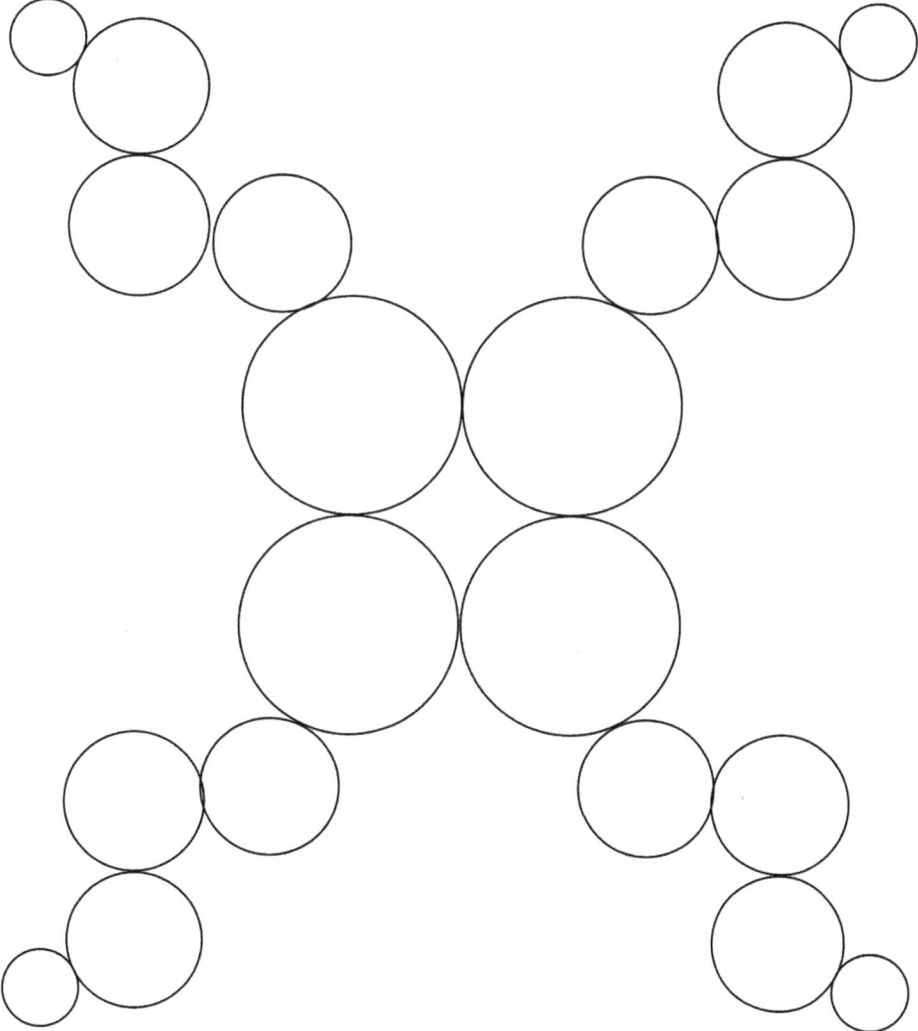

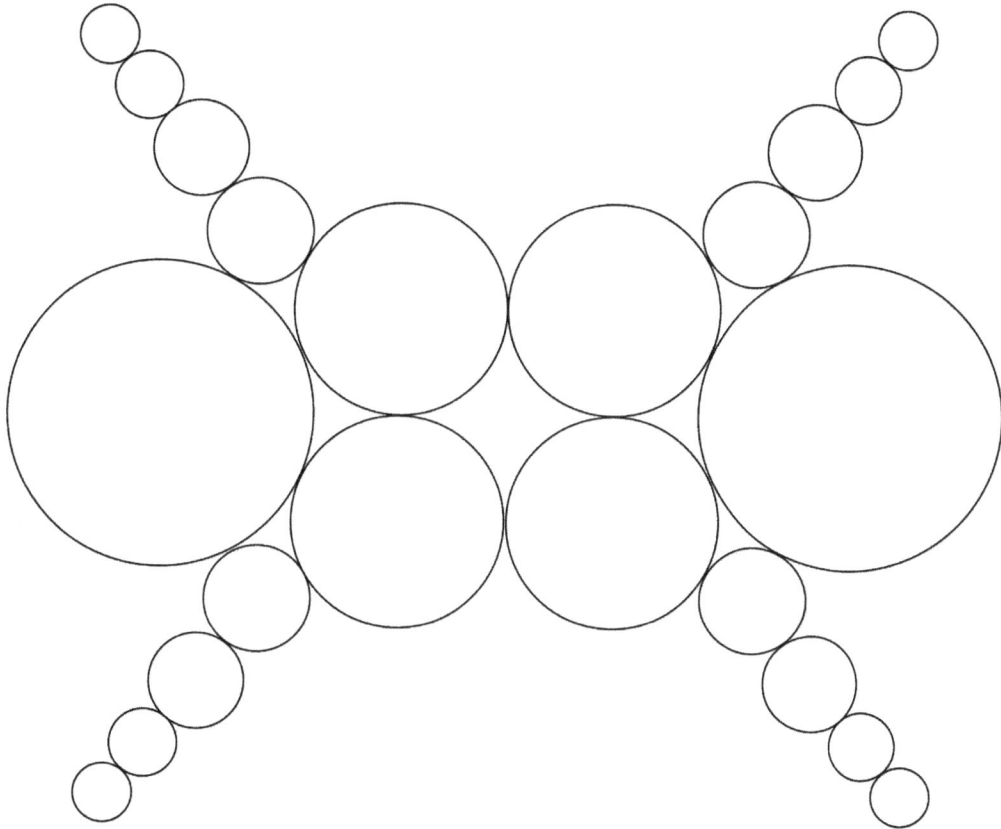

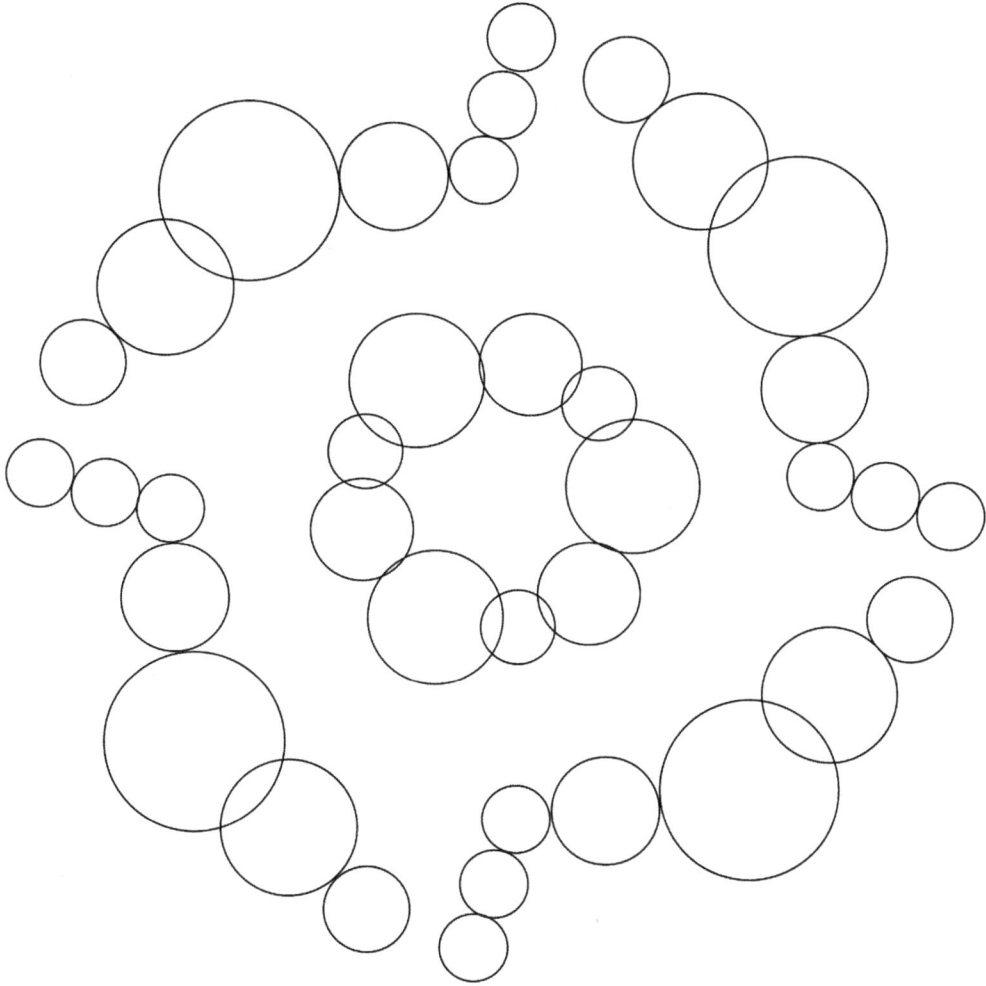

Reference Graph 11B

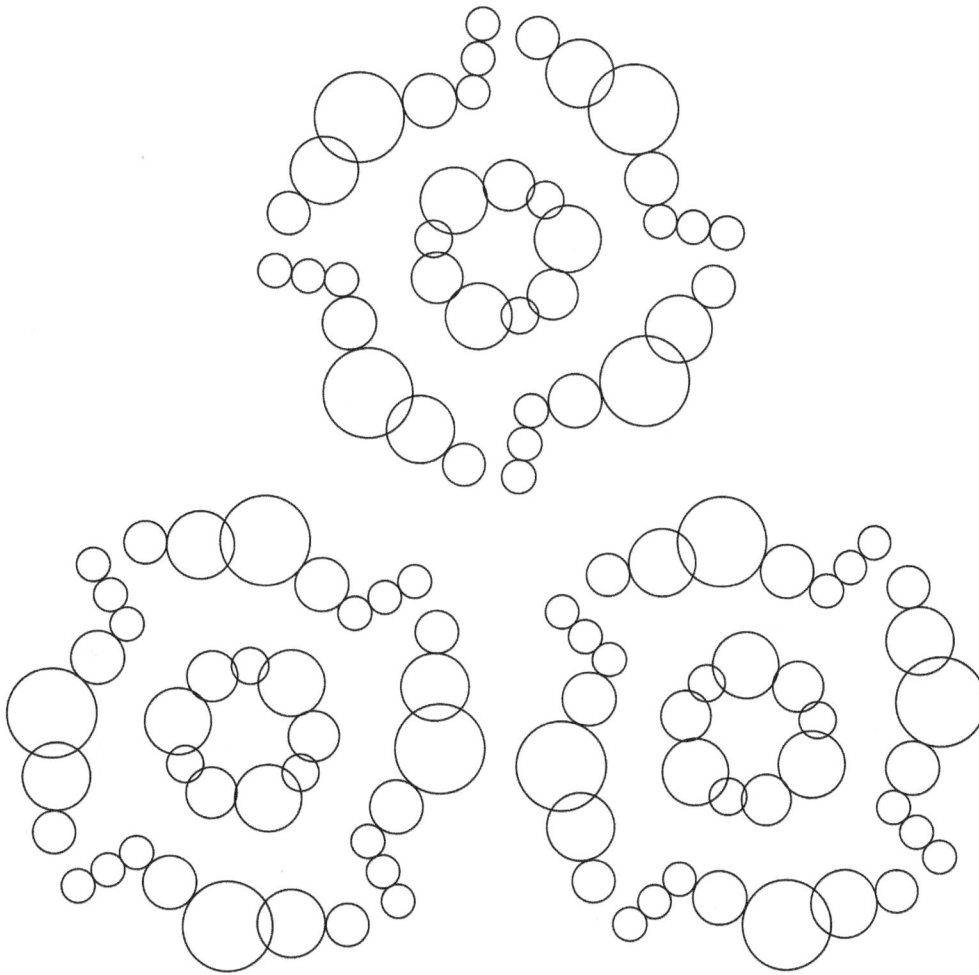

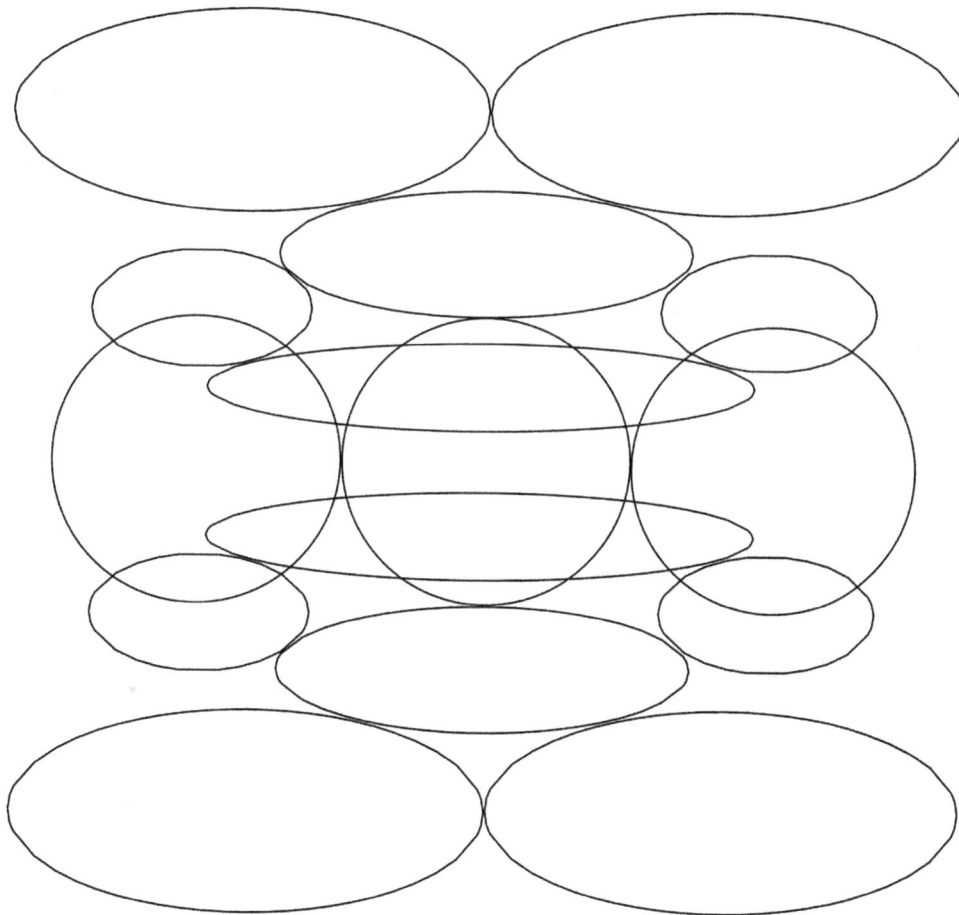

Reference Graph 12B

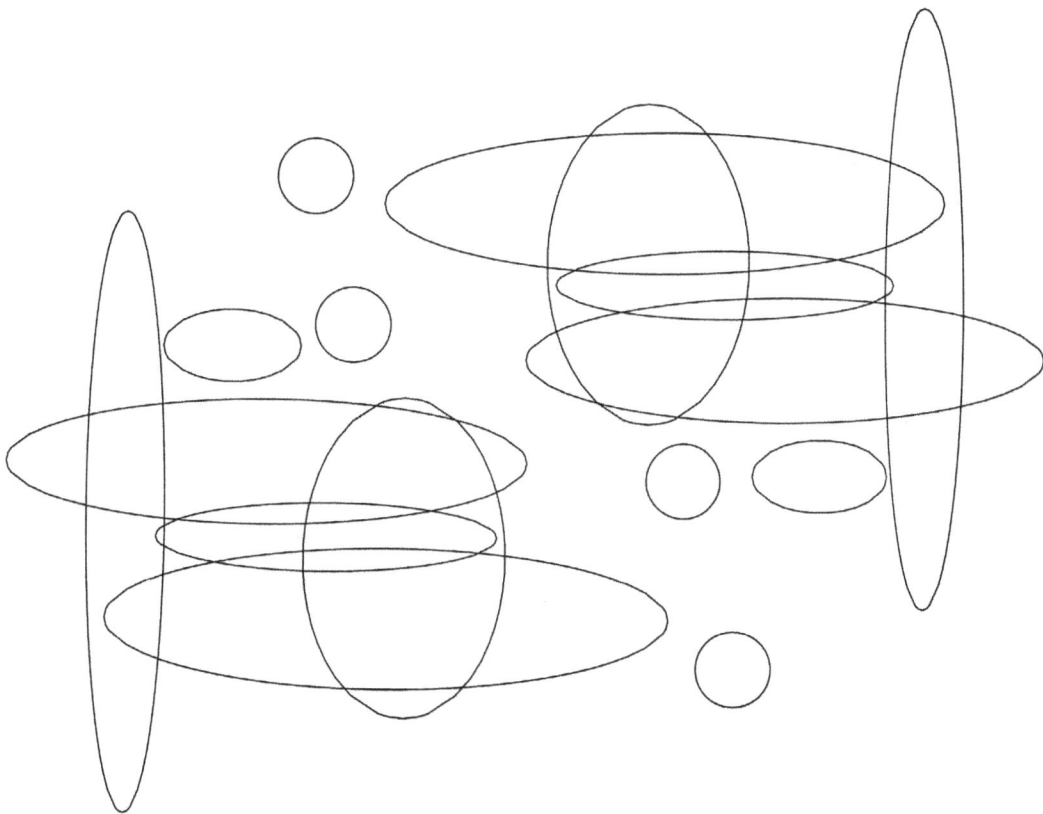

Reference Graph 14A

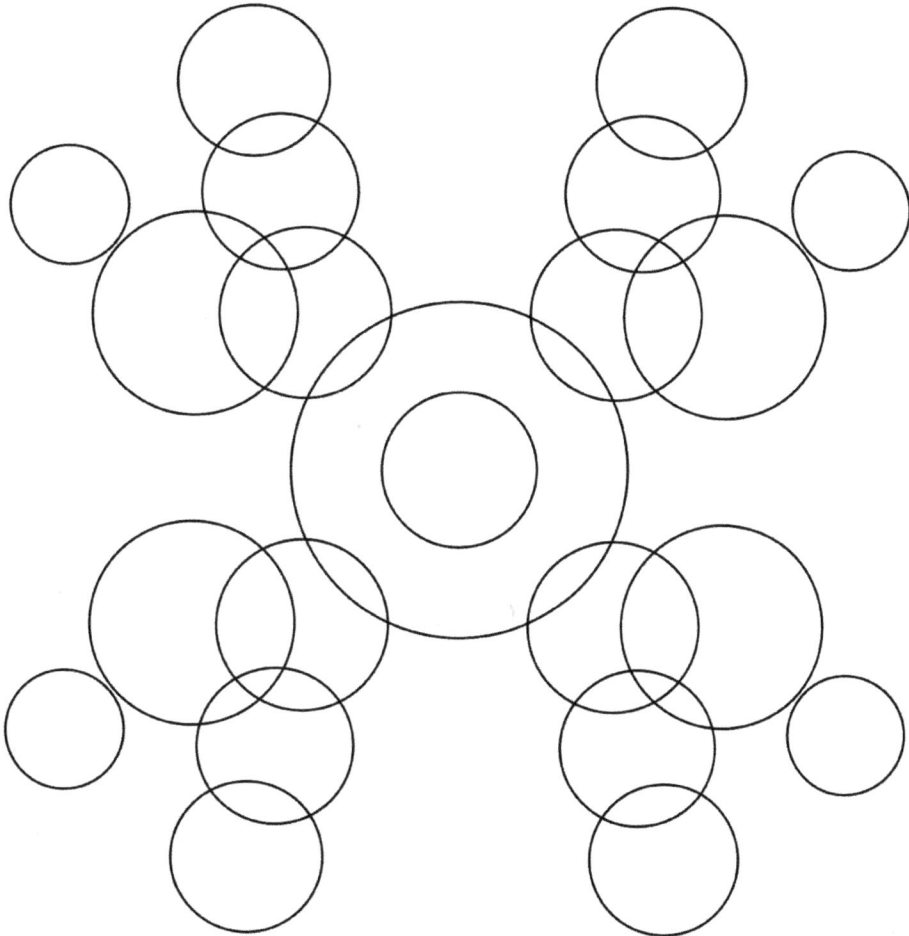

61

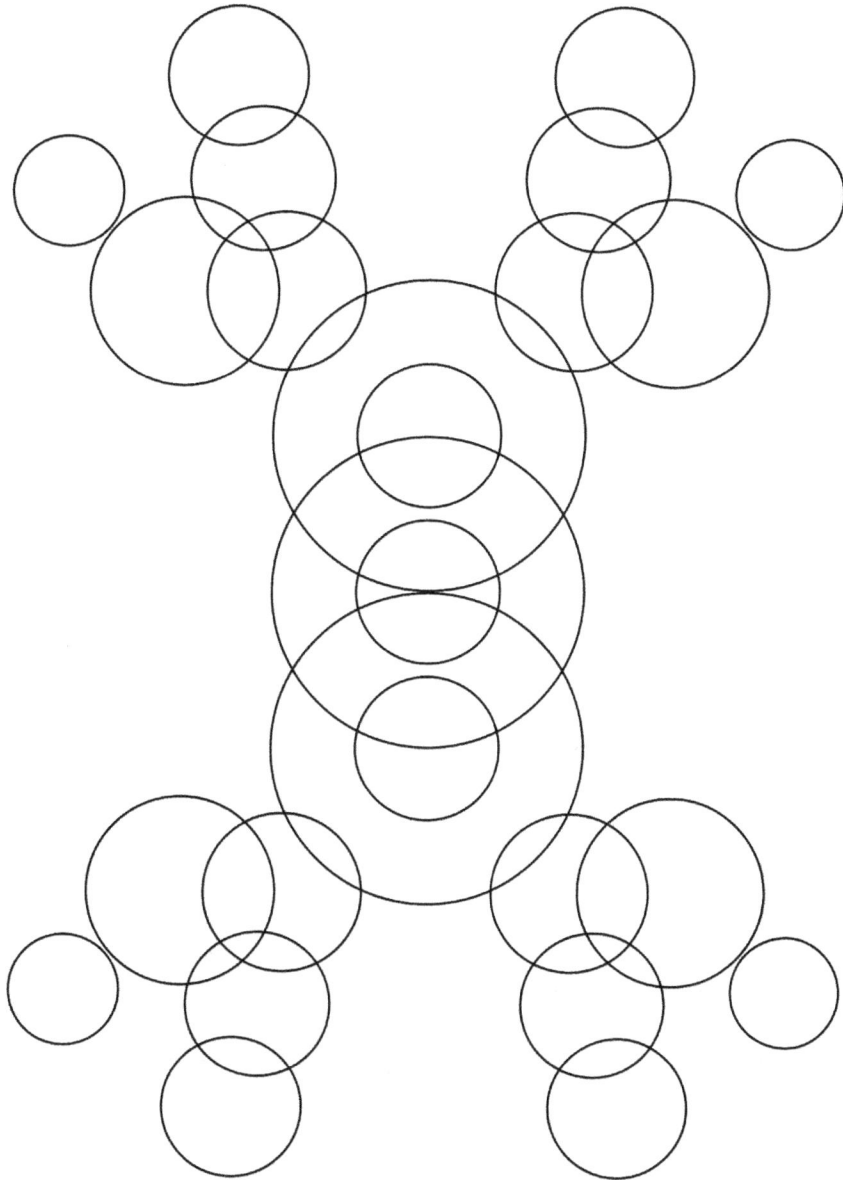

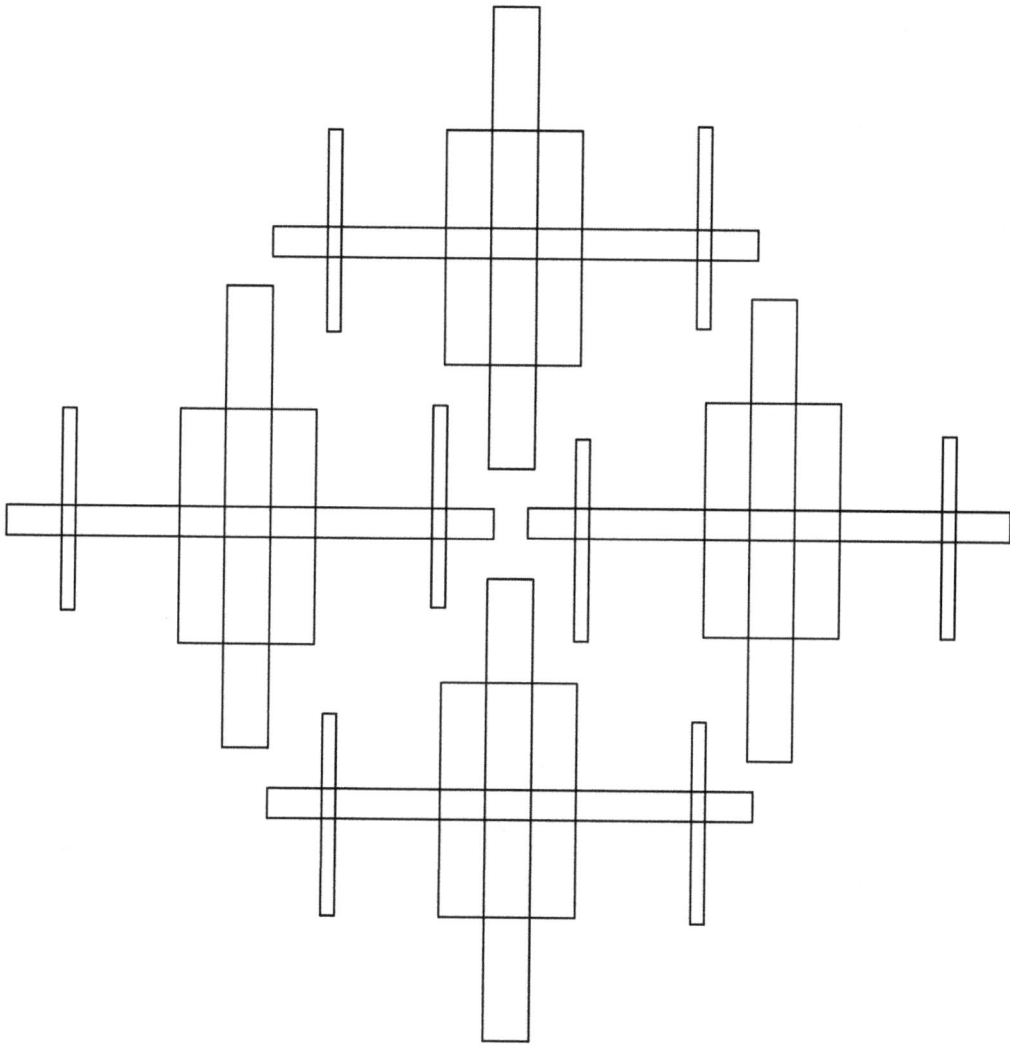

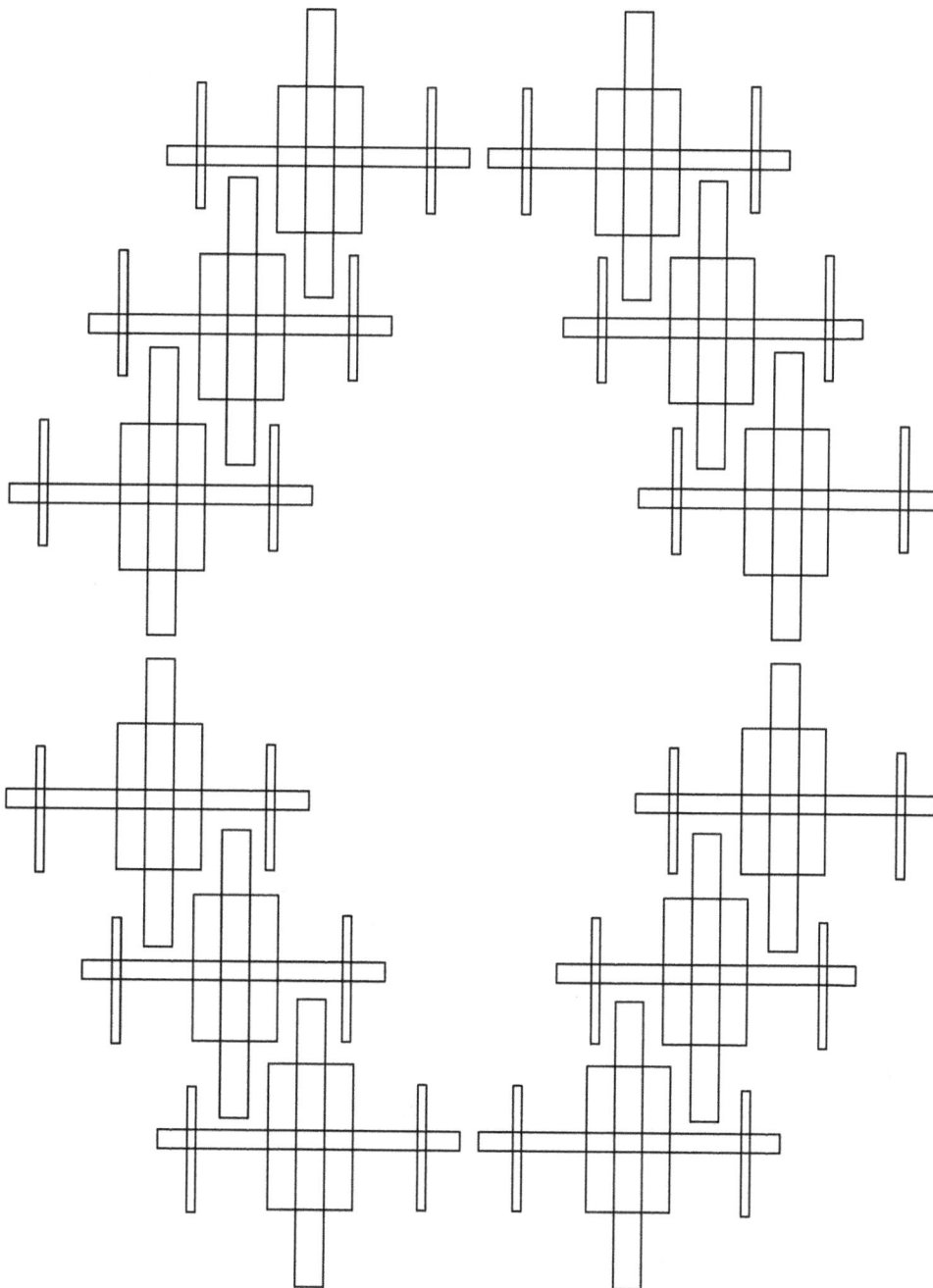

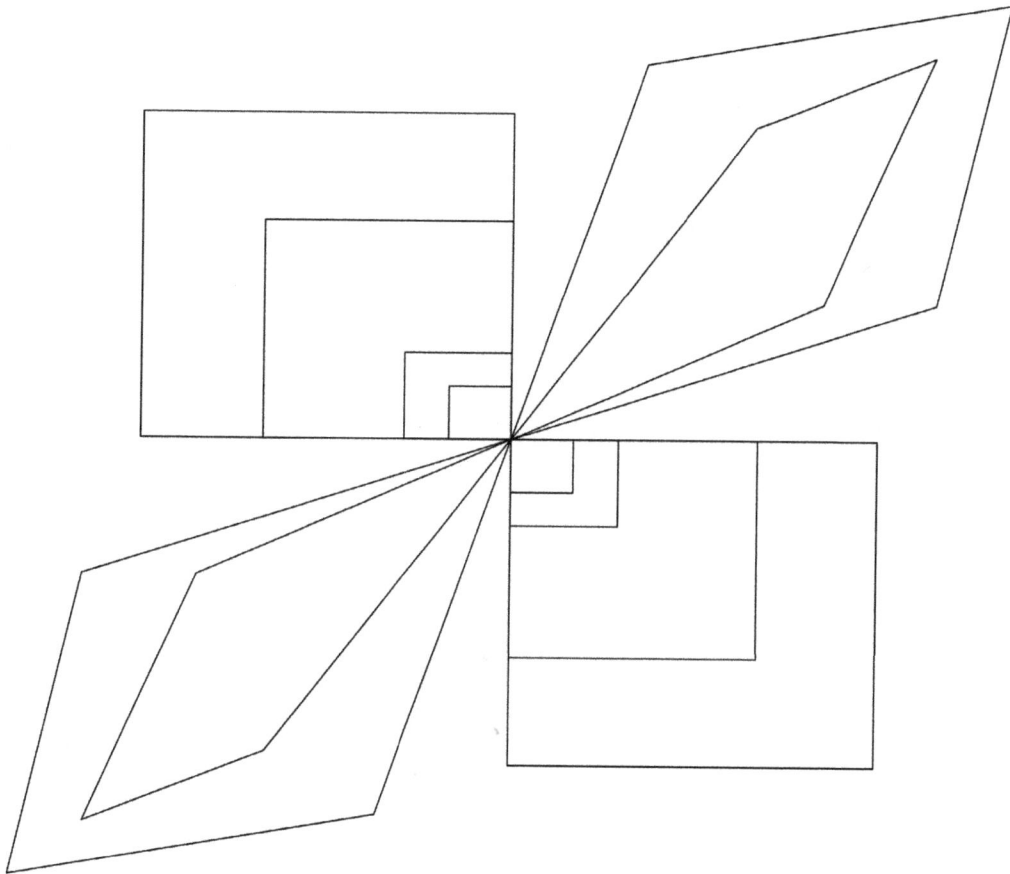

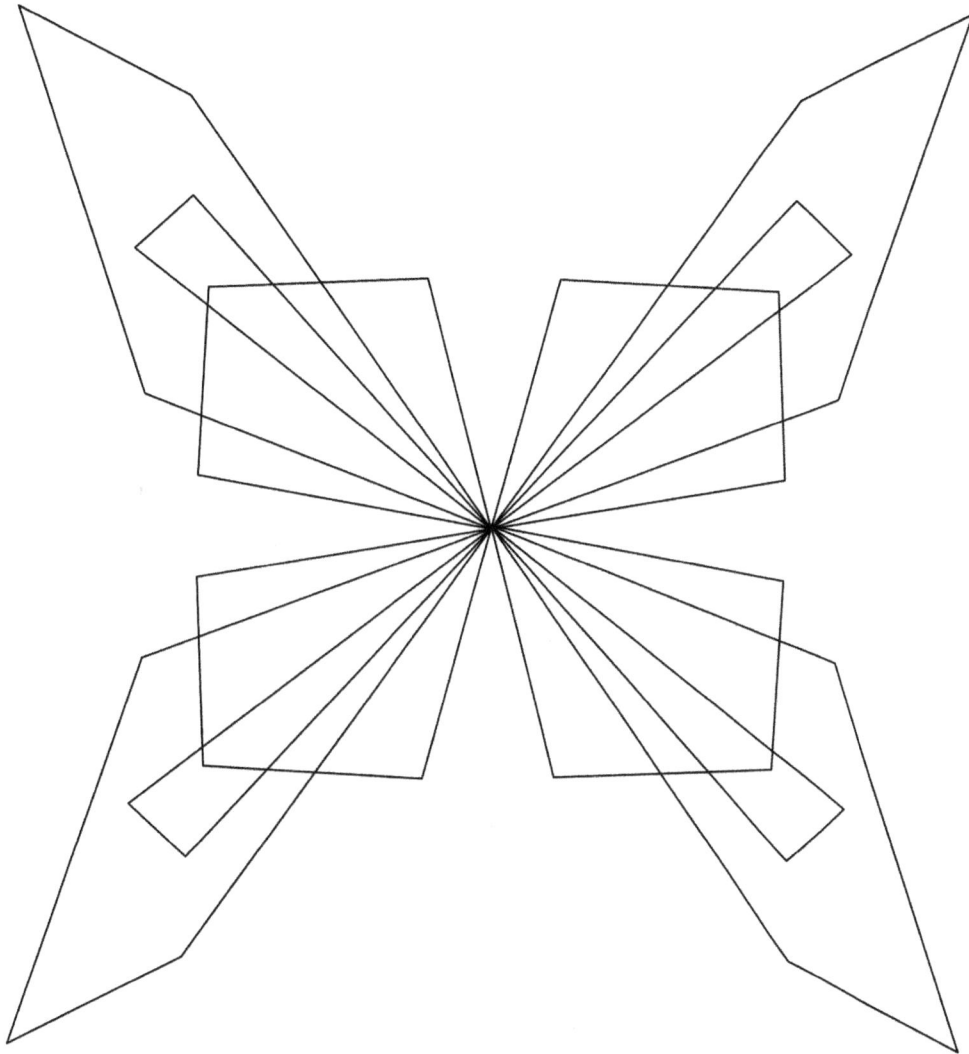

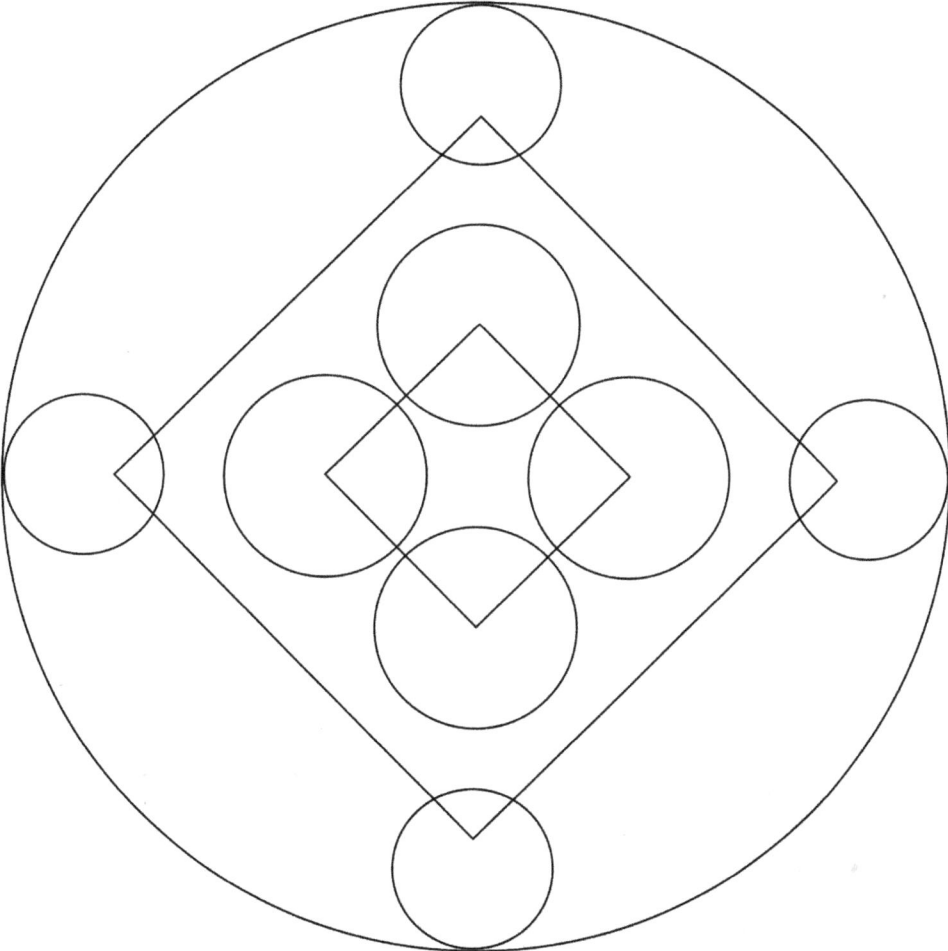

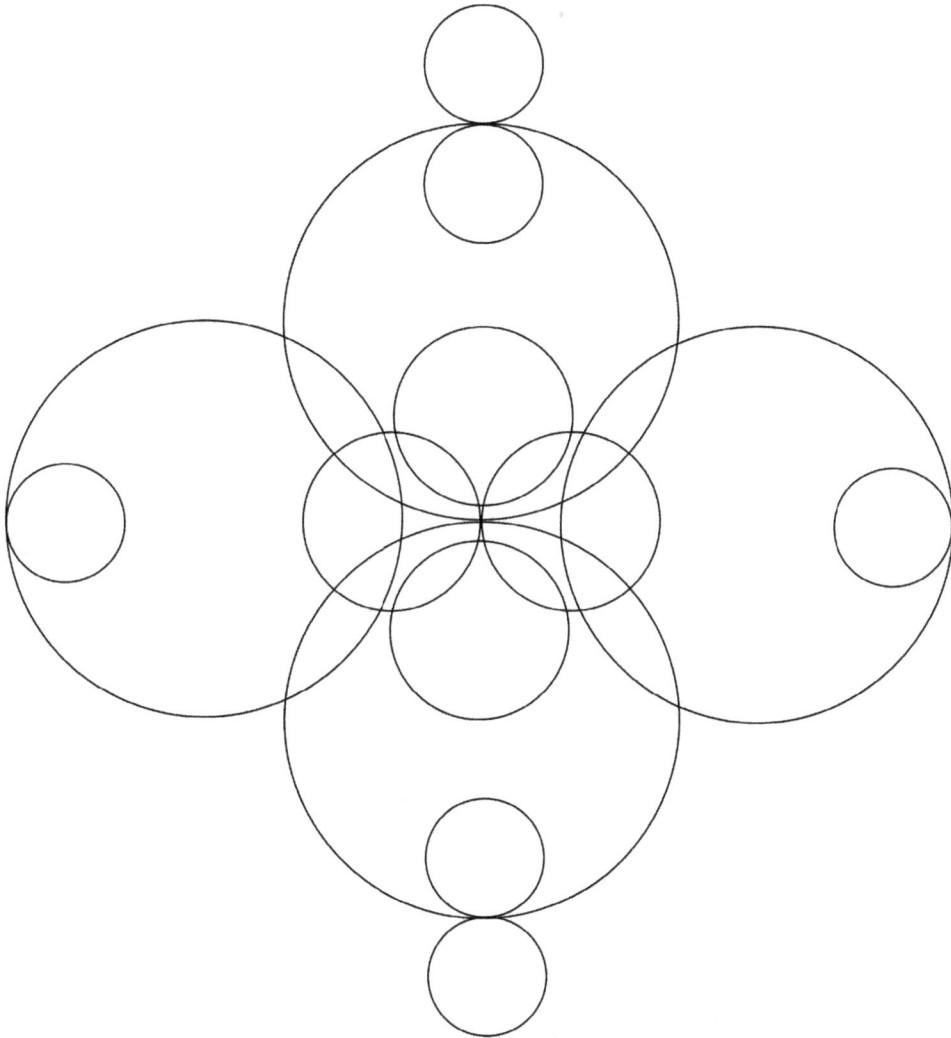

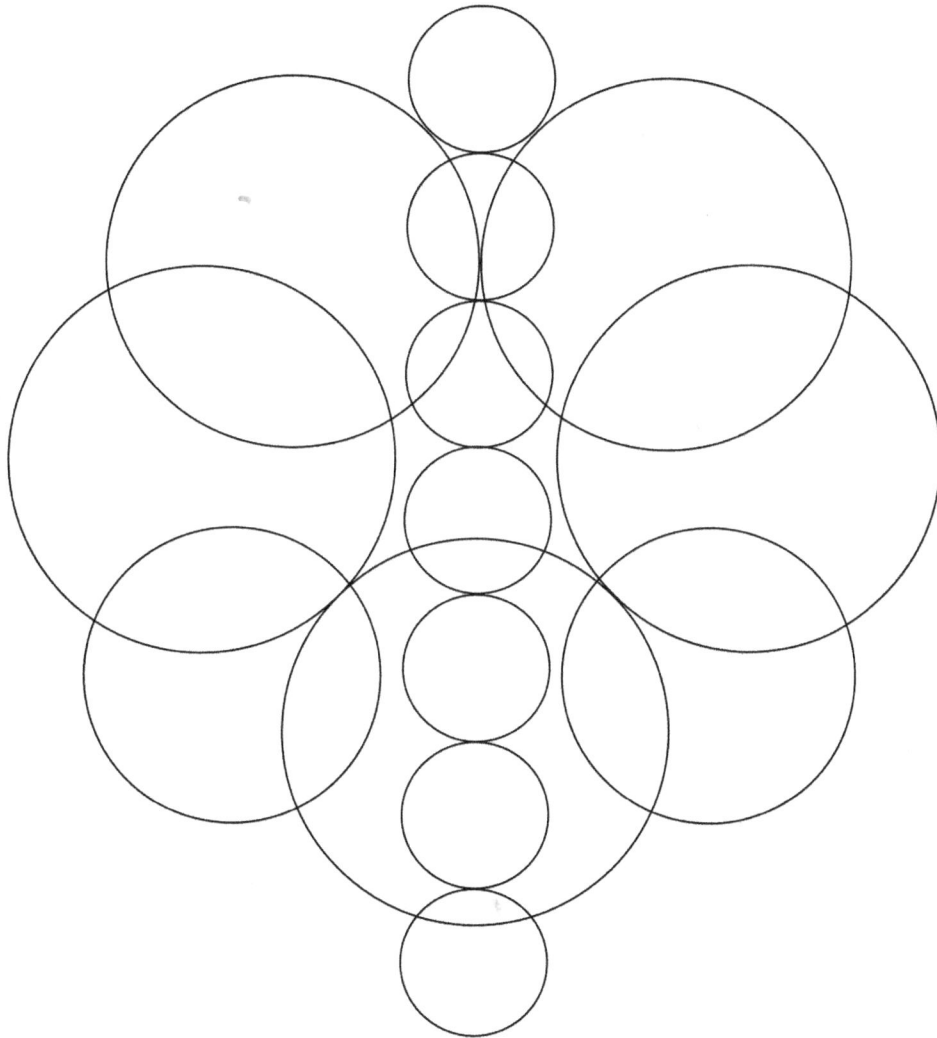

Reference Graph 19A

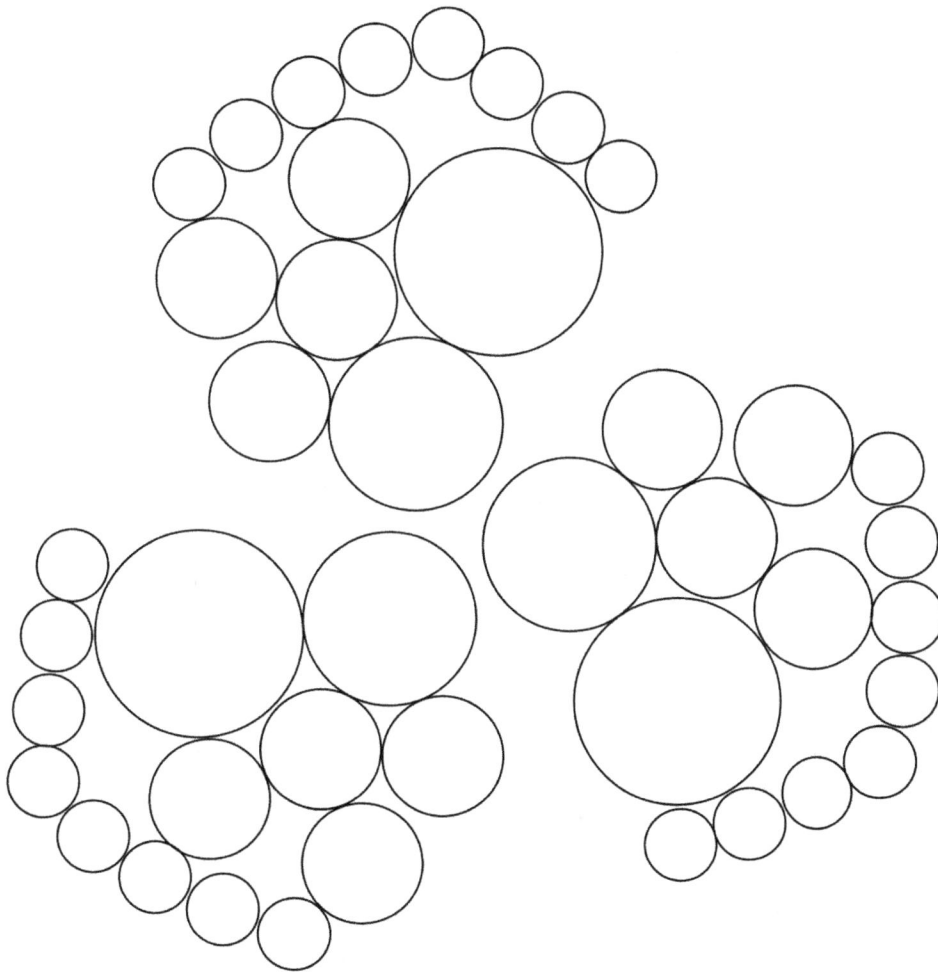

81

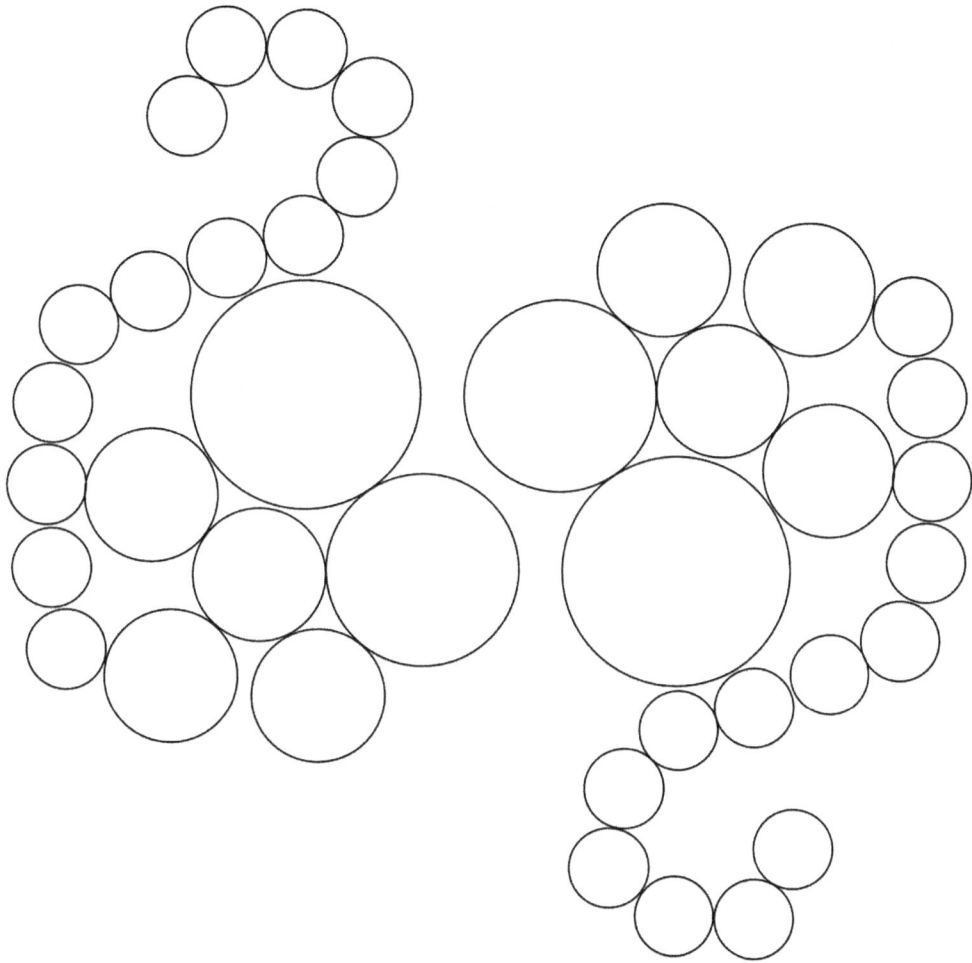

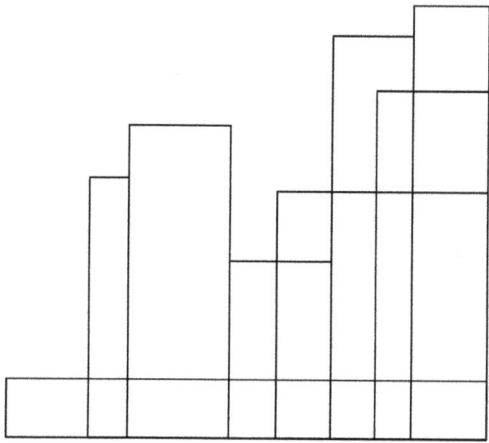

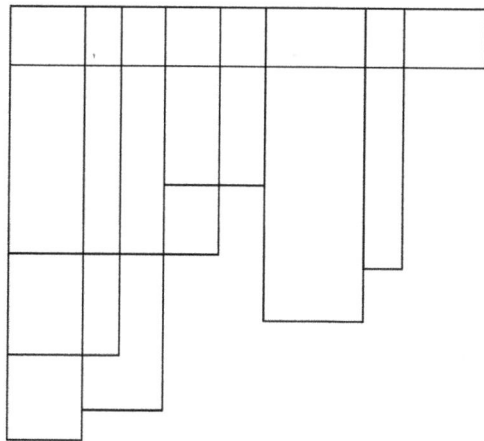

Reference Graph 20B

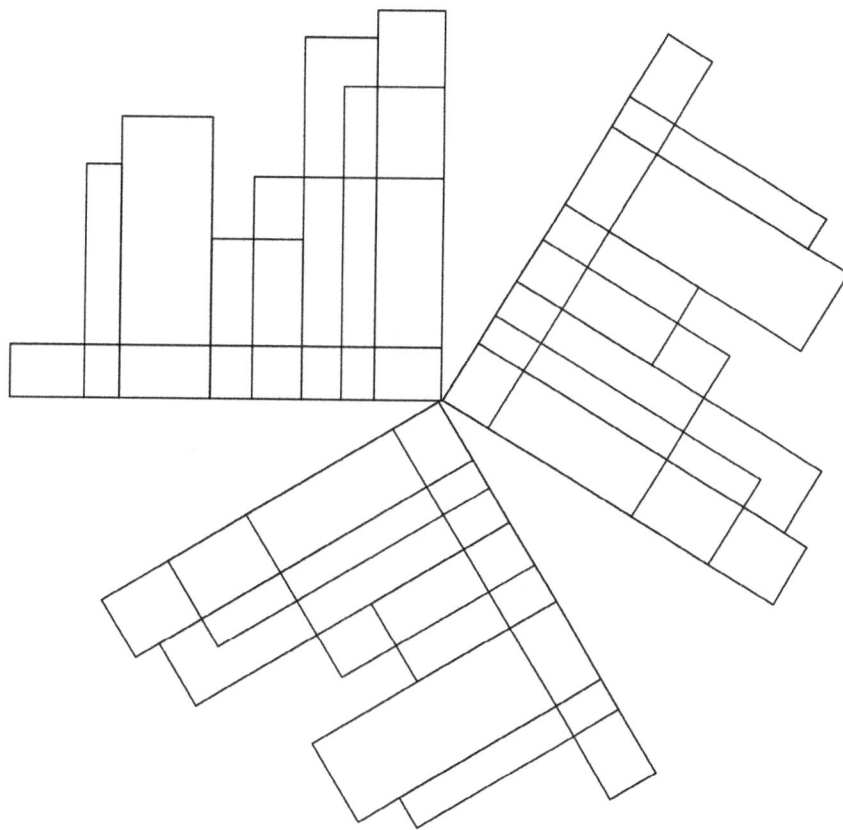

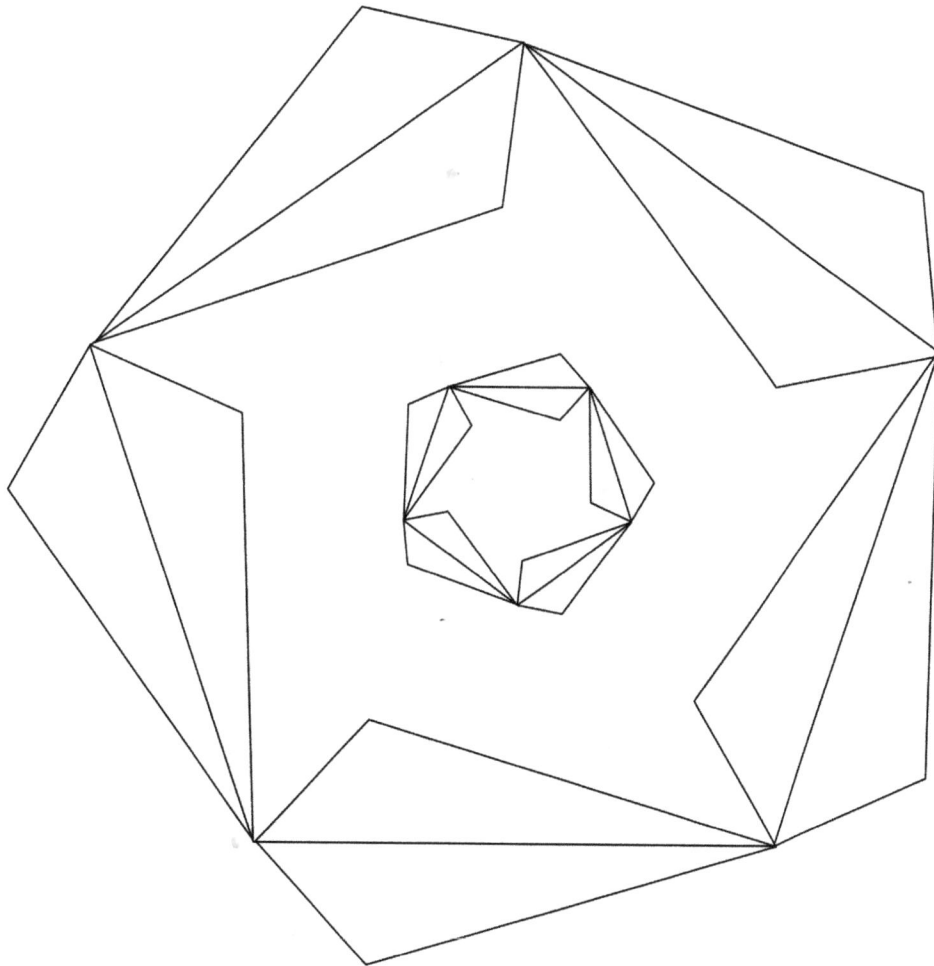

Reference Graph 21B

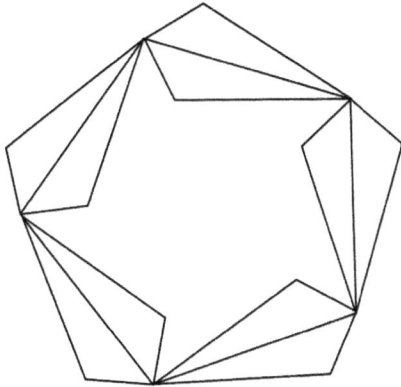

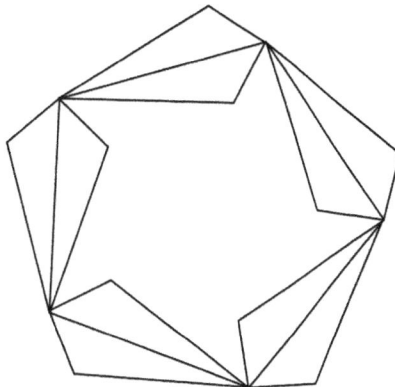

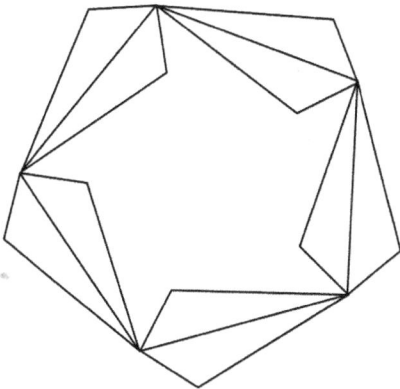

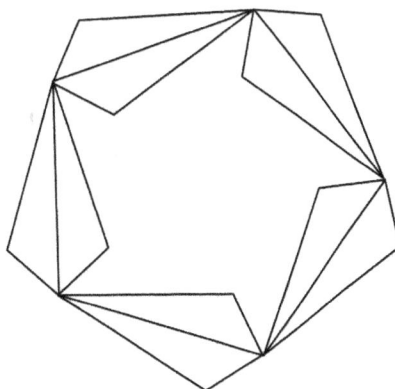

91

Reference Graph 22A

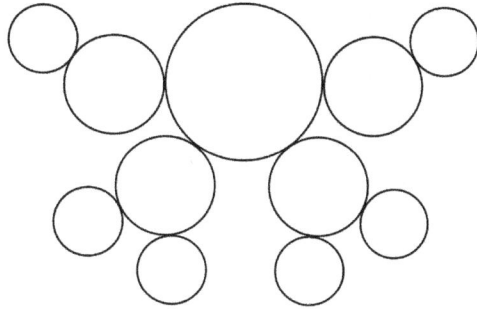

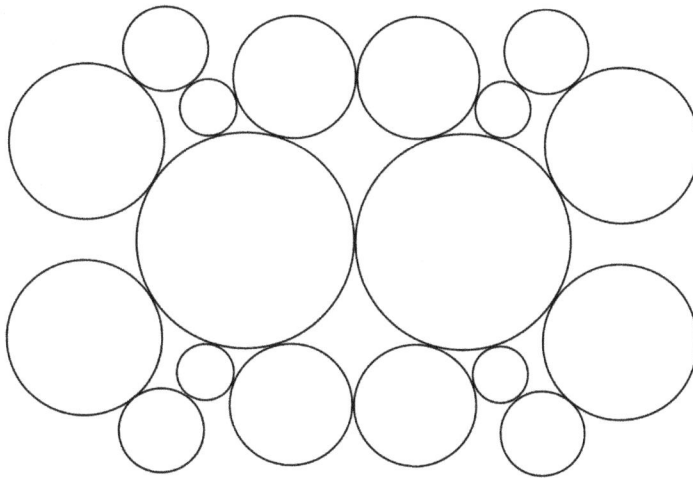

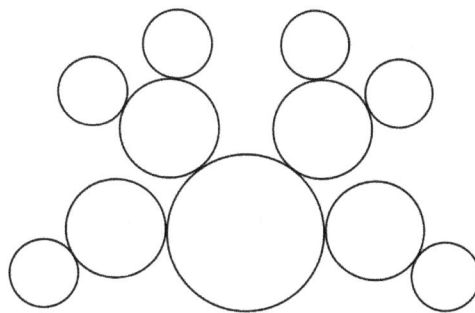

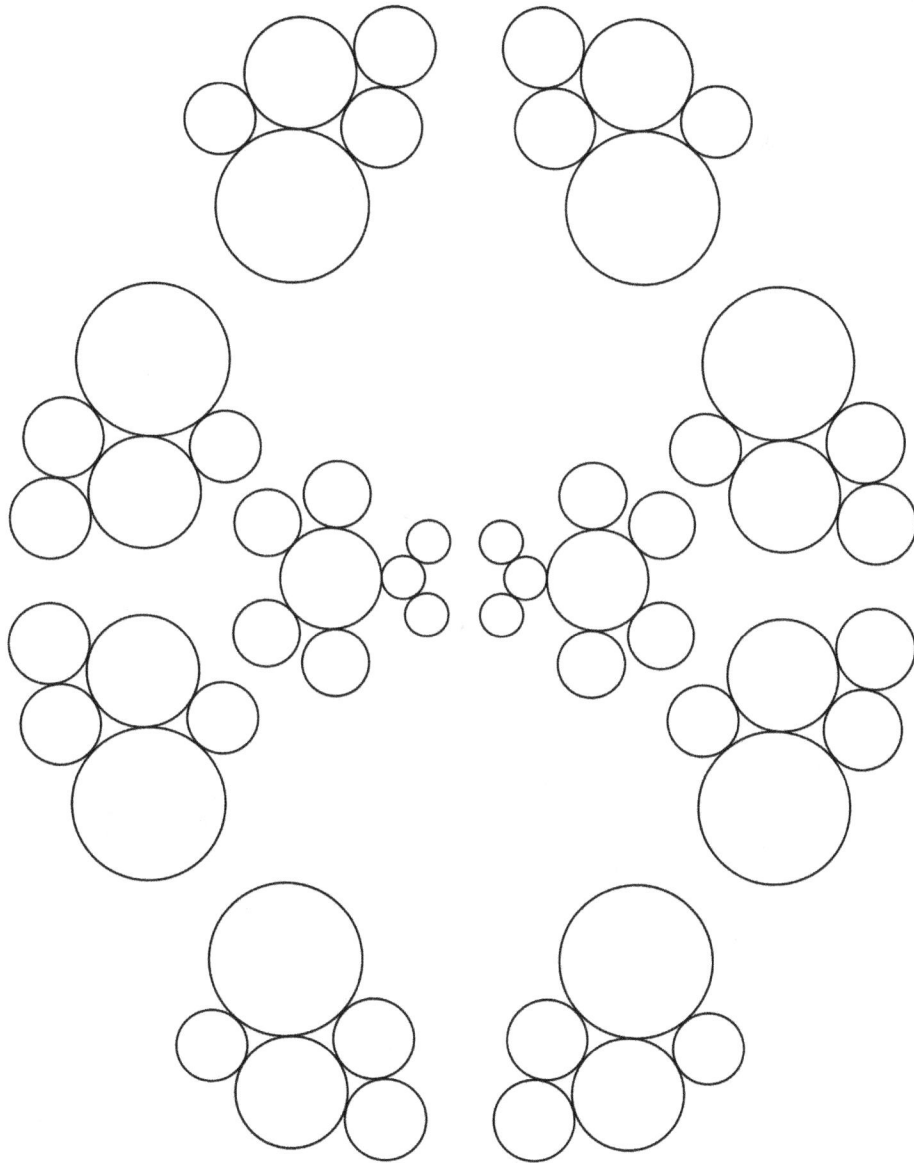

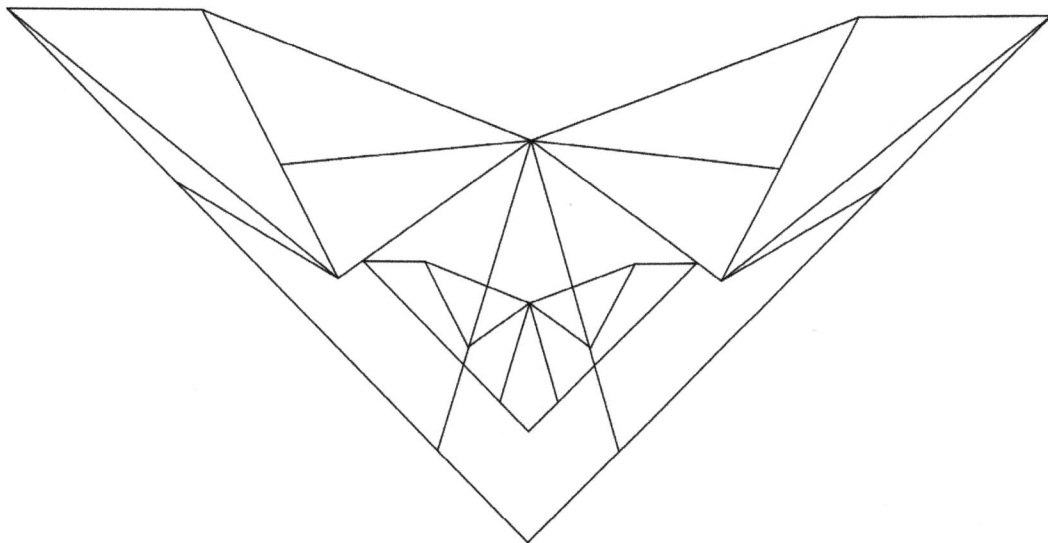

Reference Graph 23B

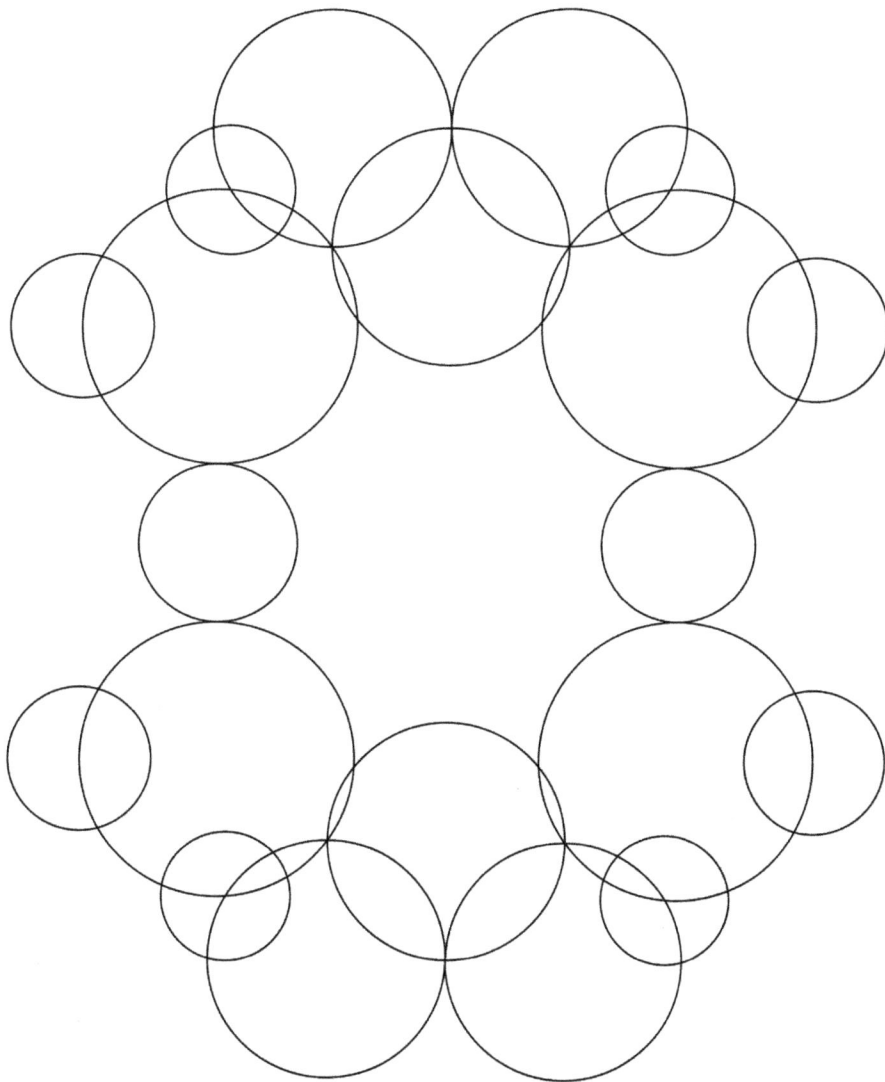

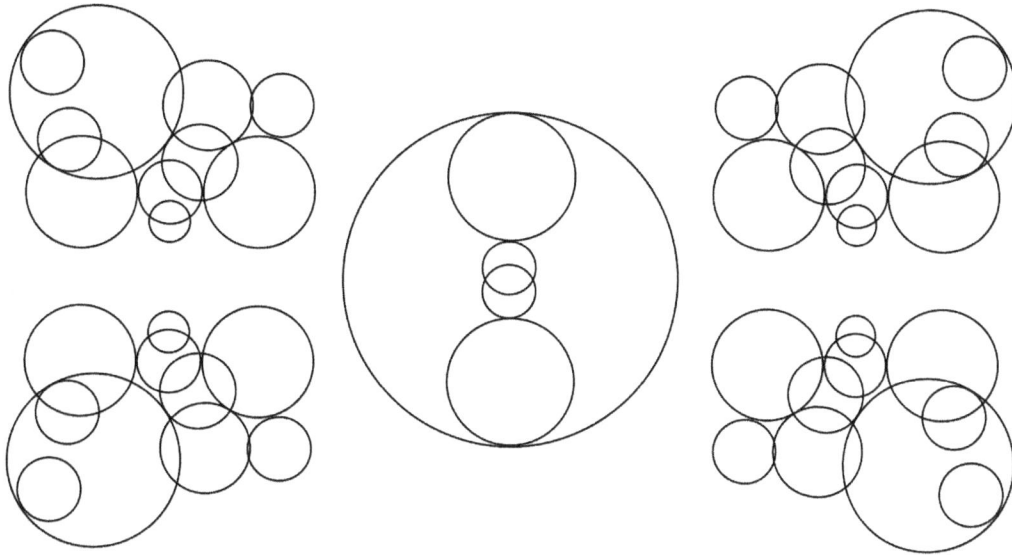

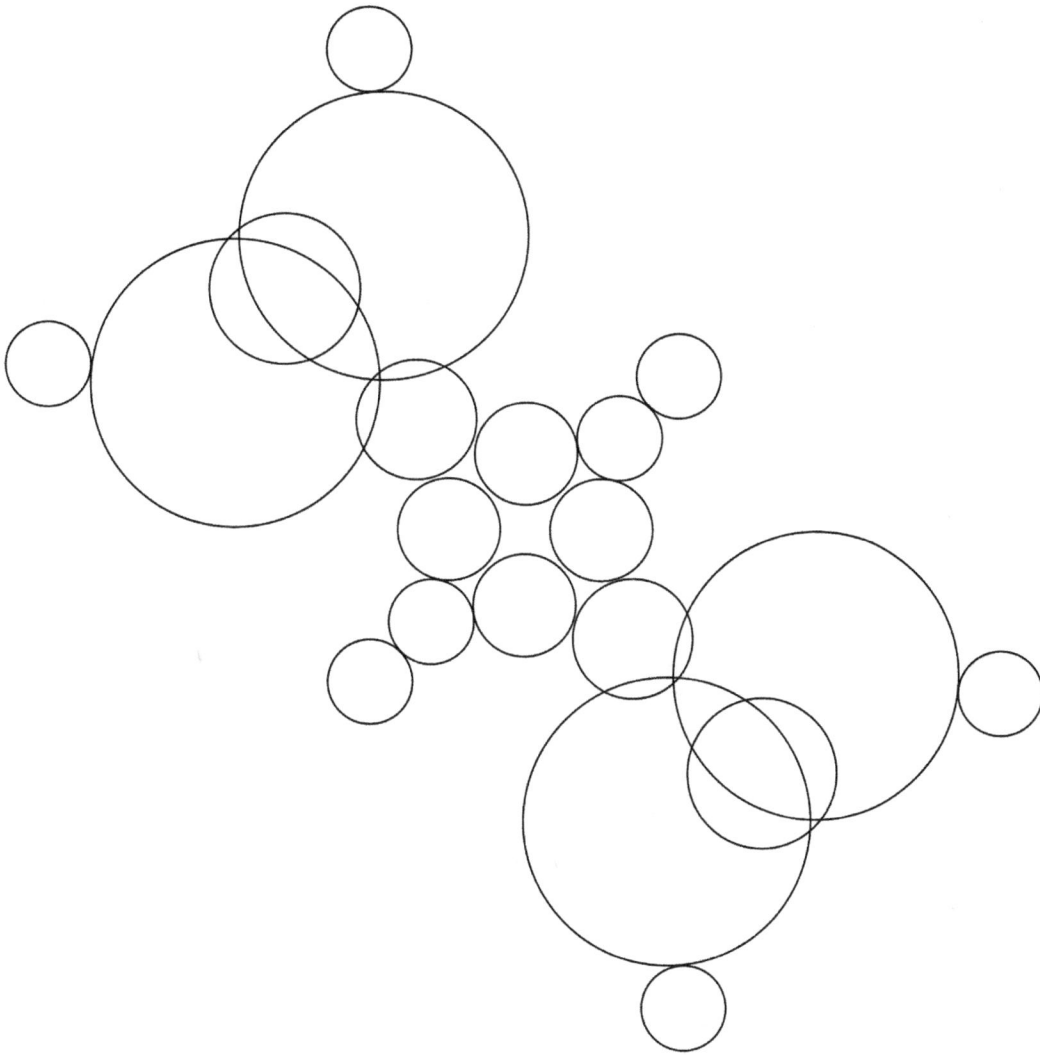

Reference Graph 25B

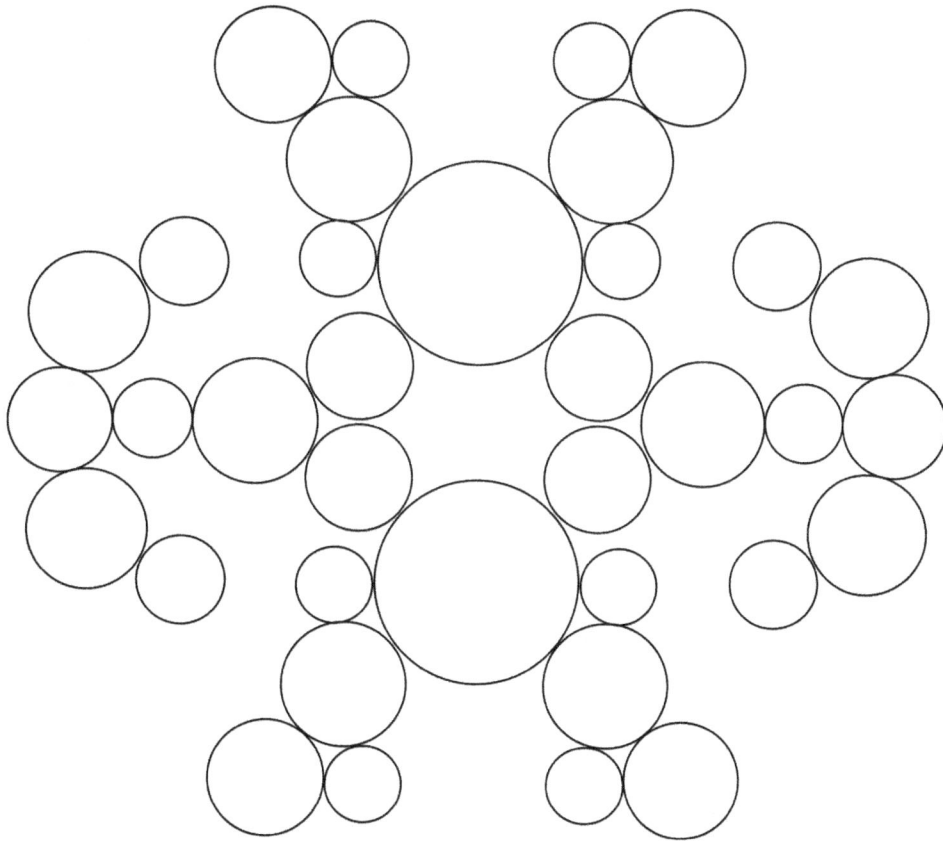

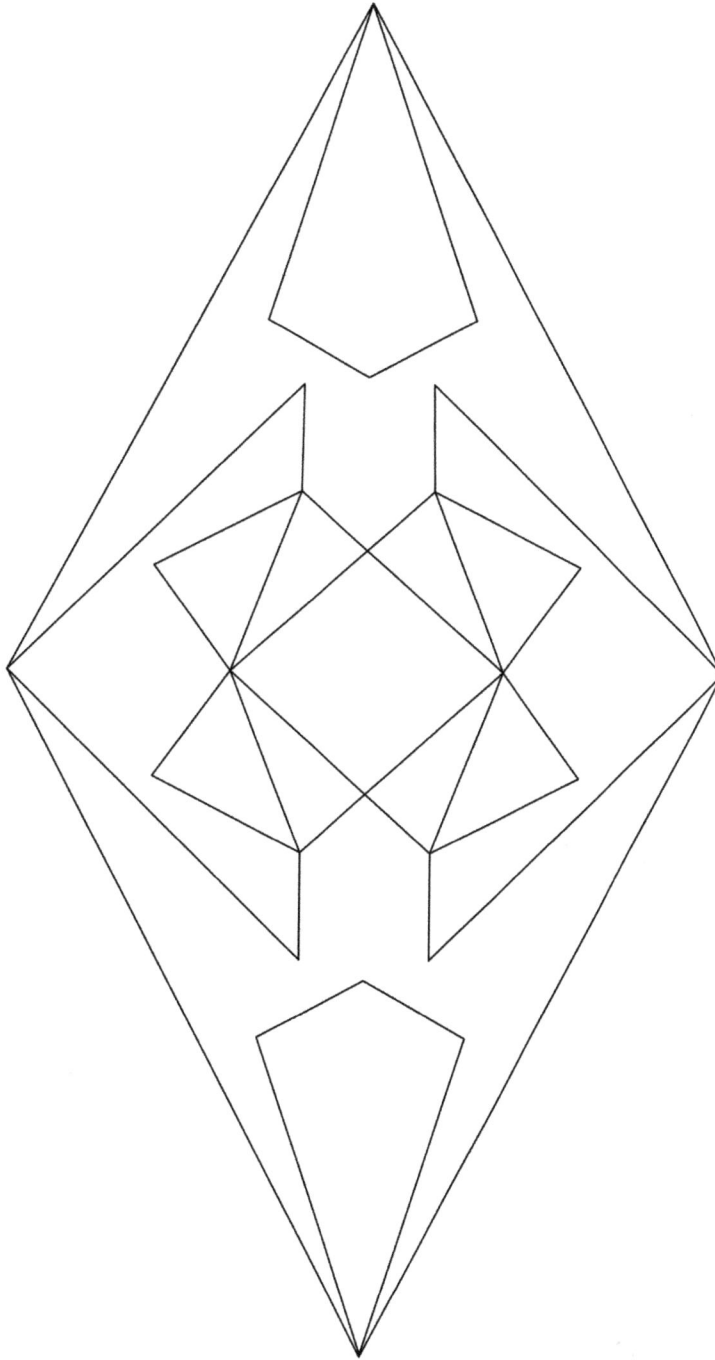

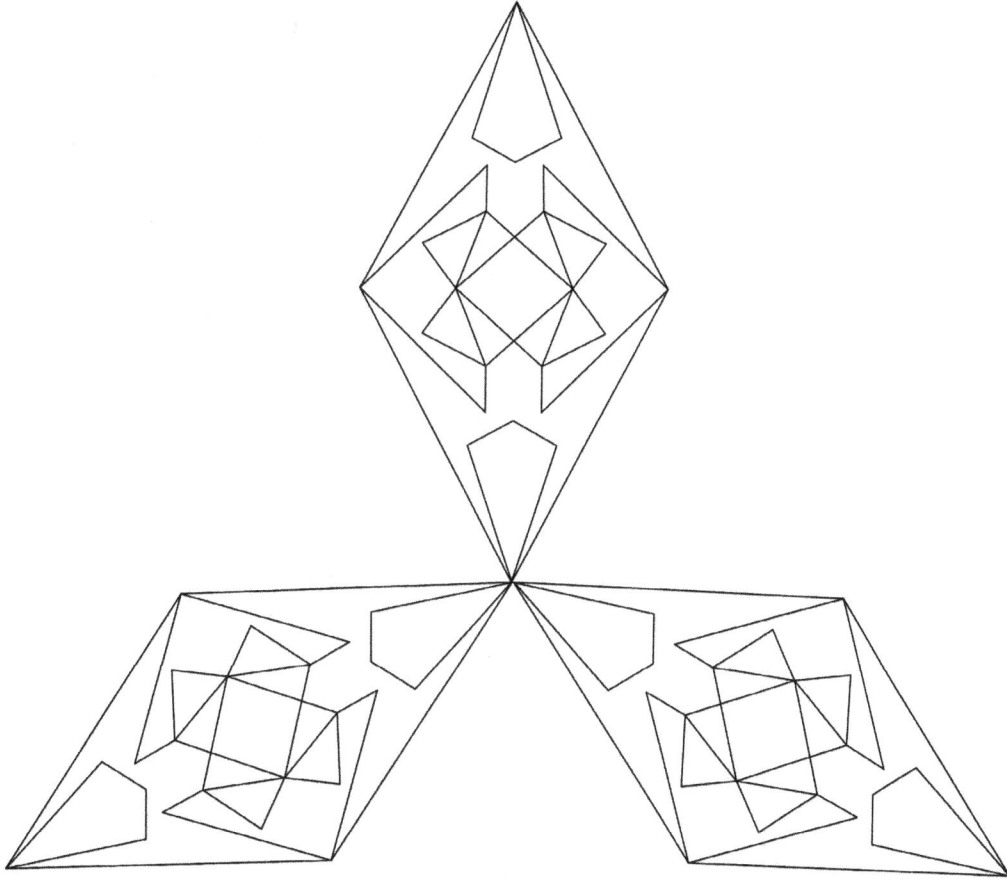

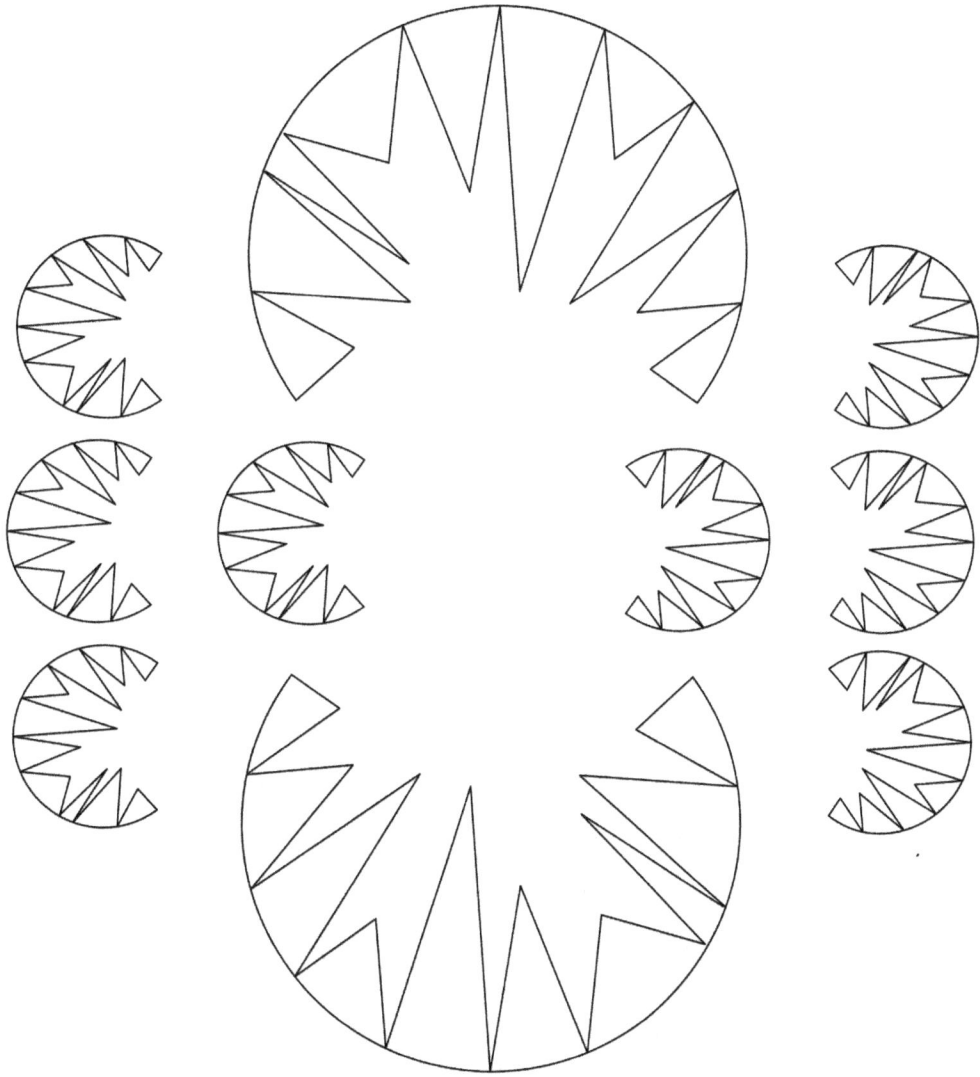

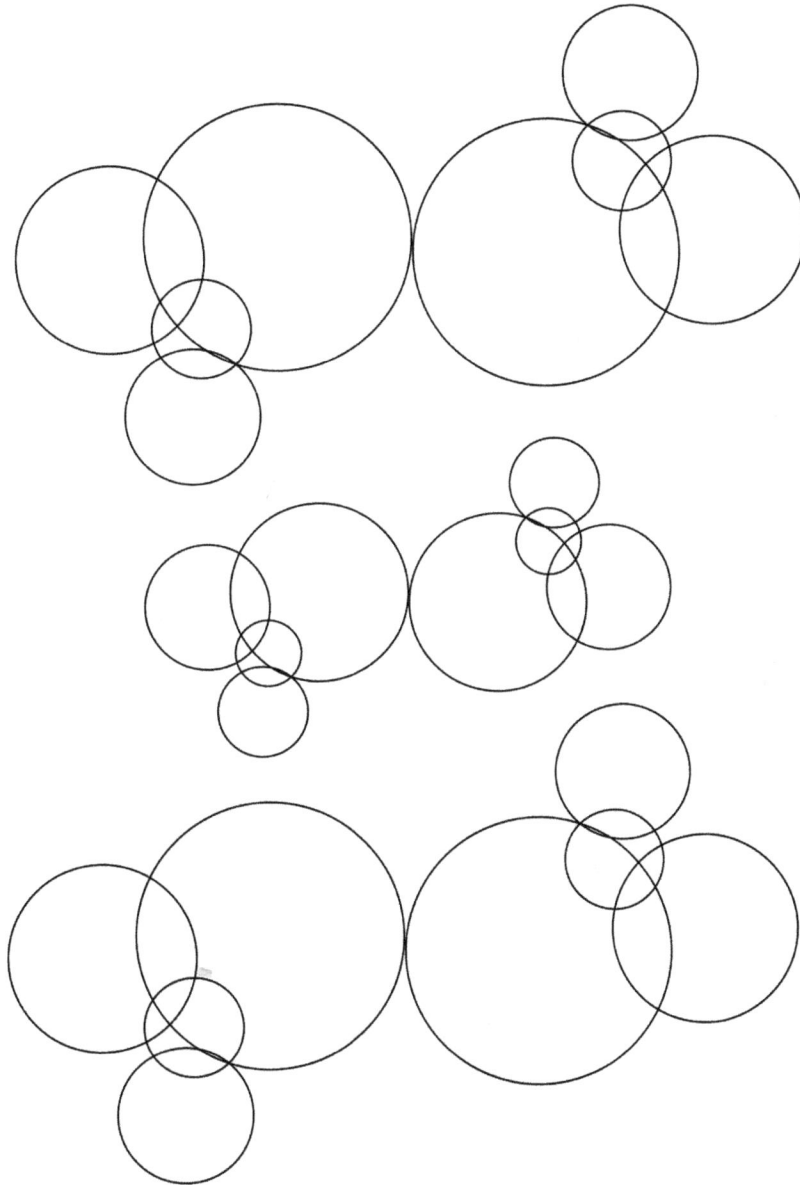

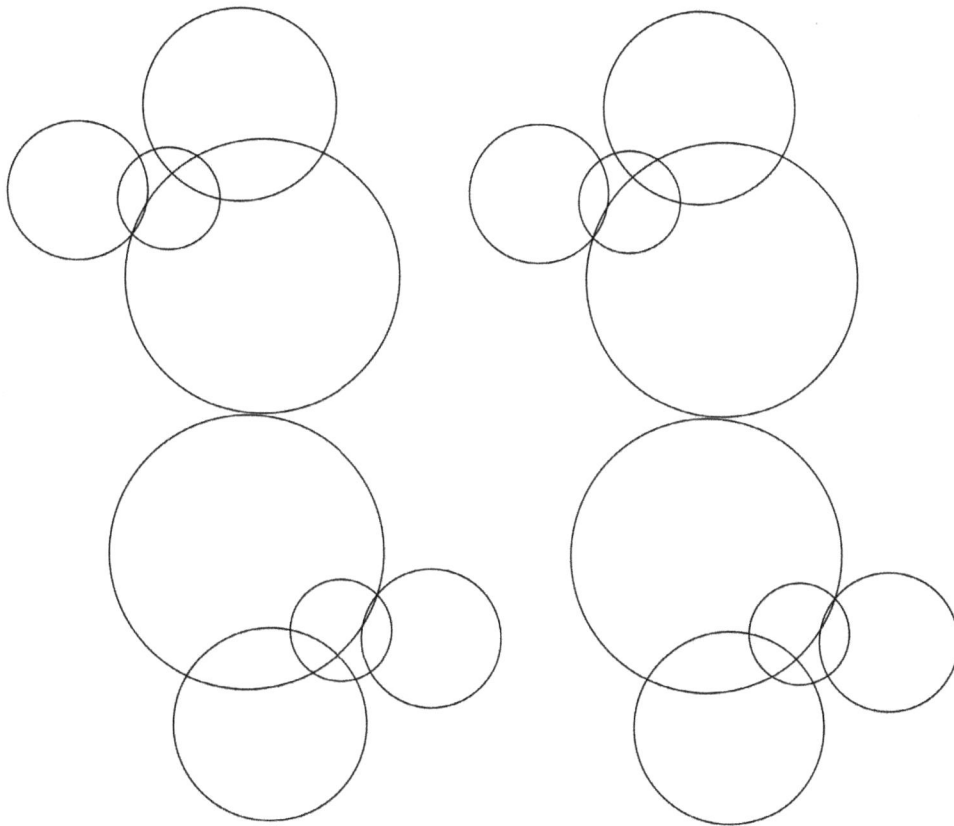

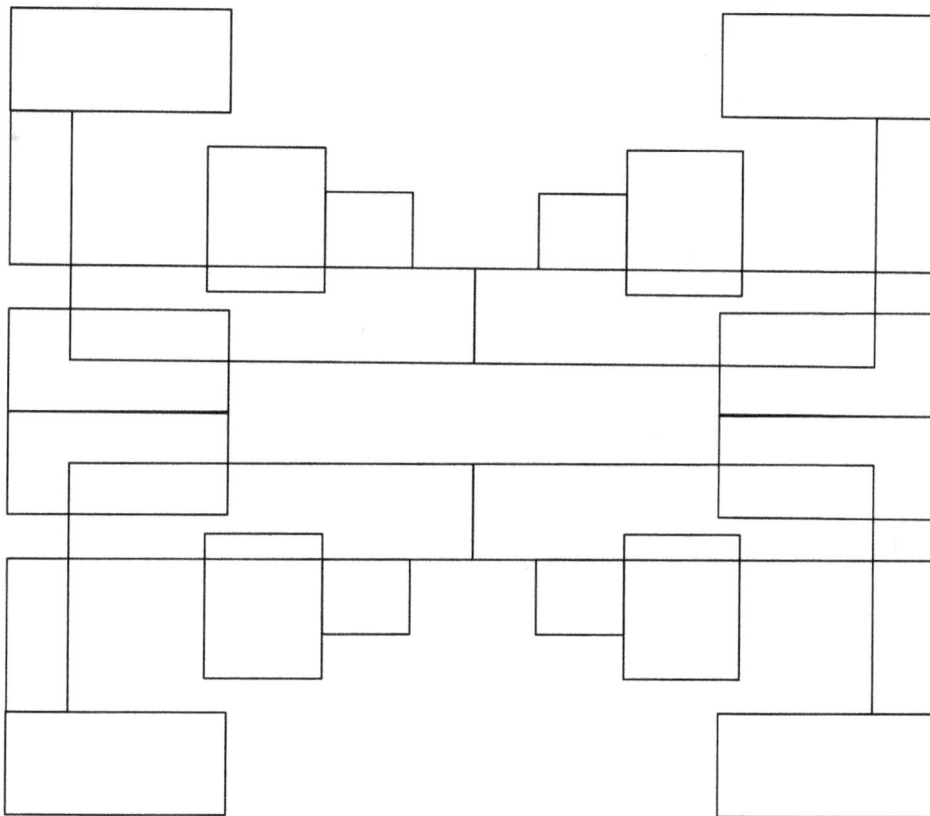

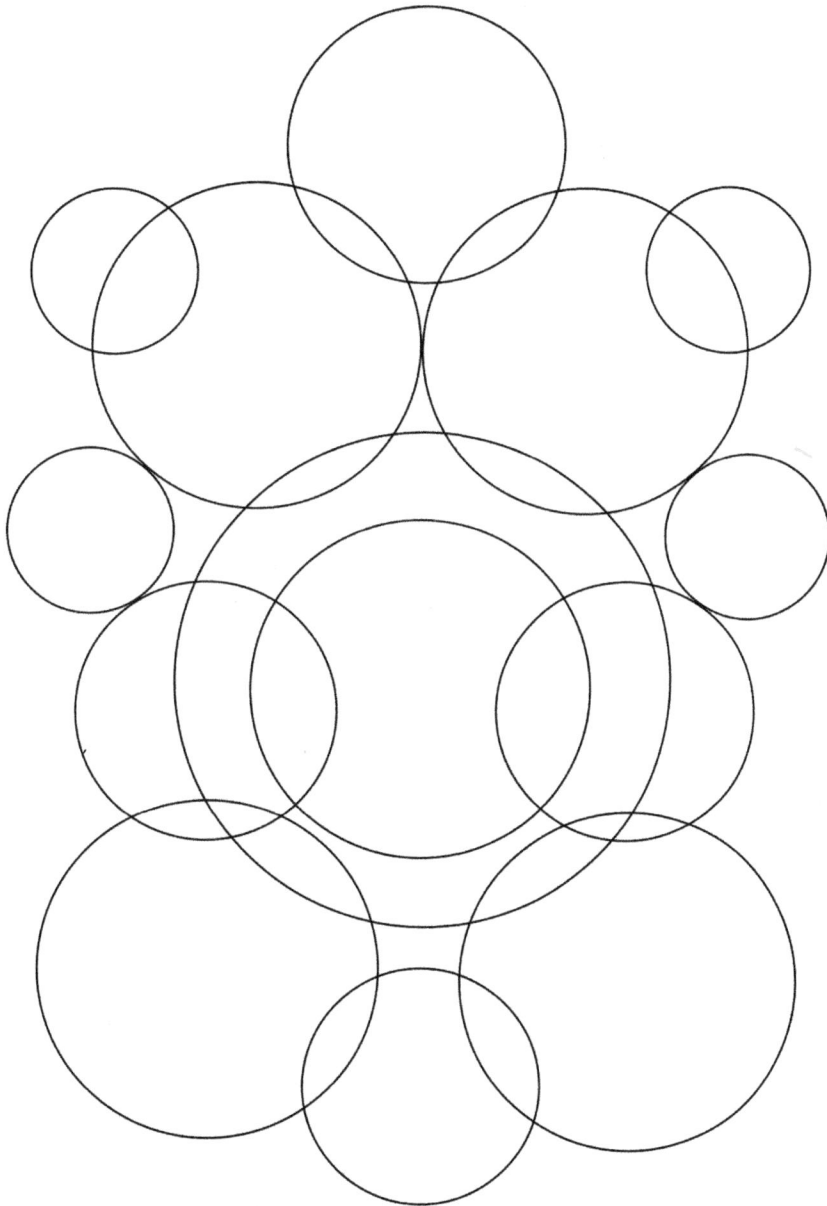

Reference Graph 30B

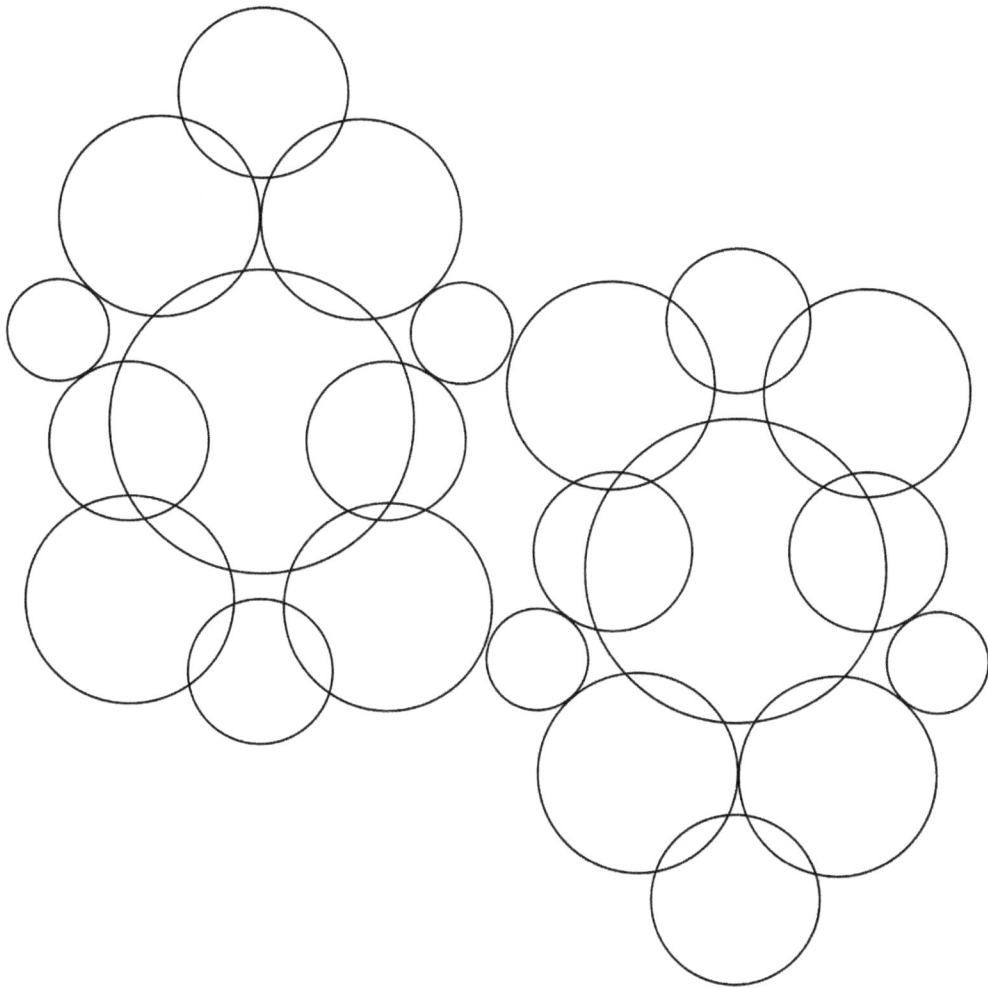

Reference Graph 31A

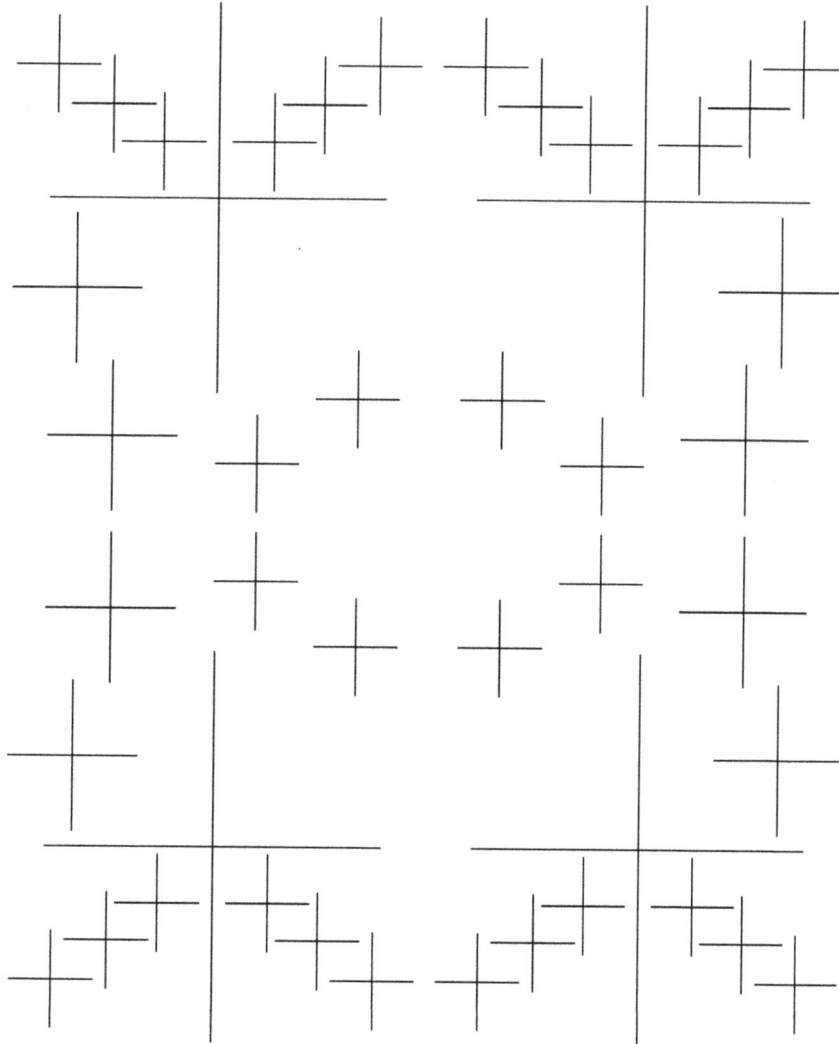

129

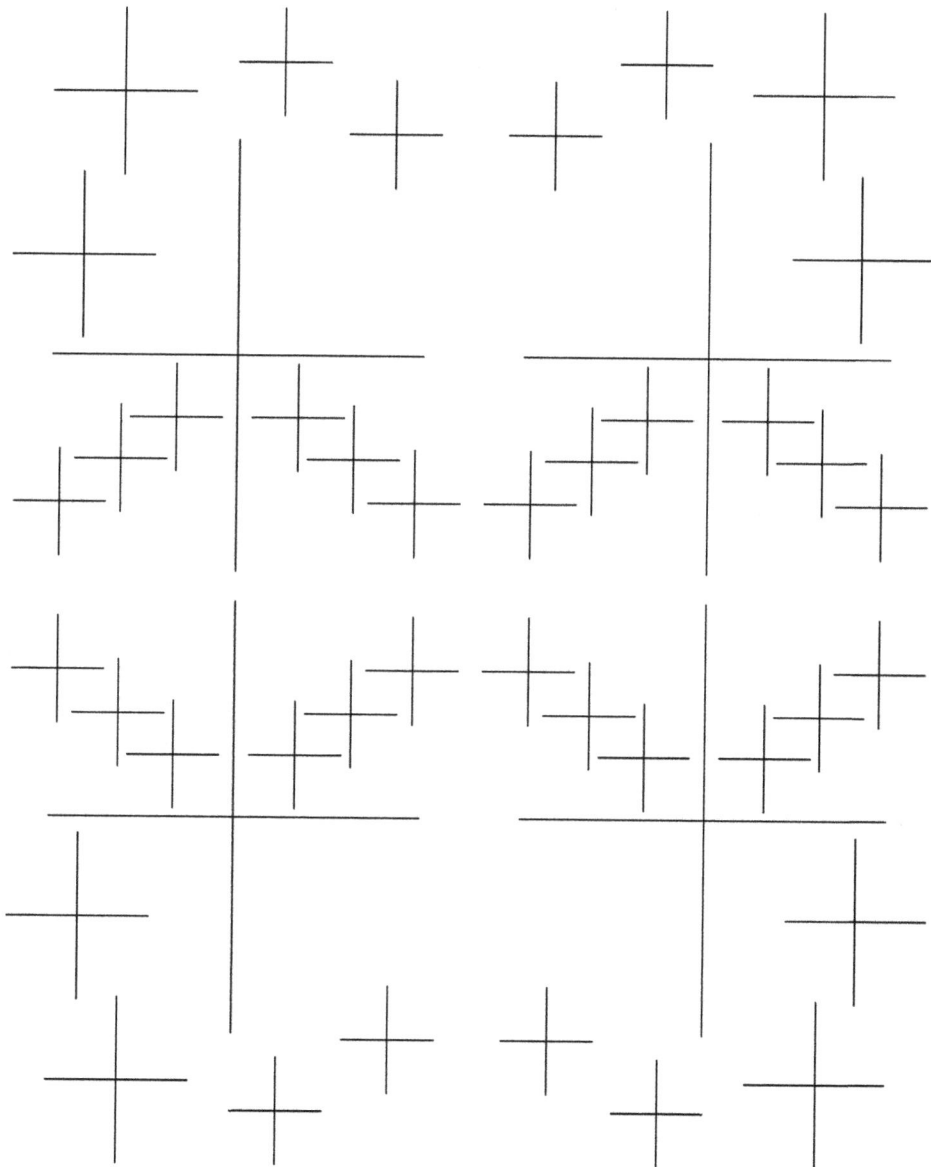

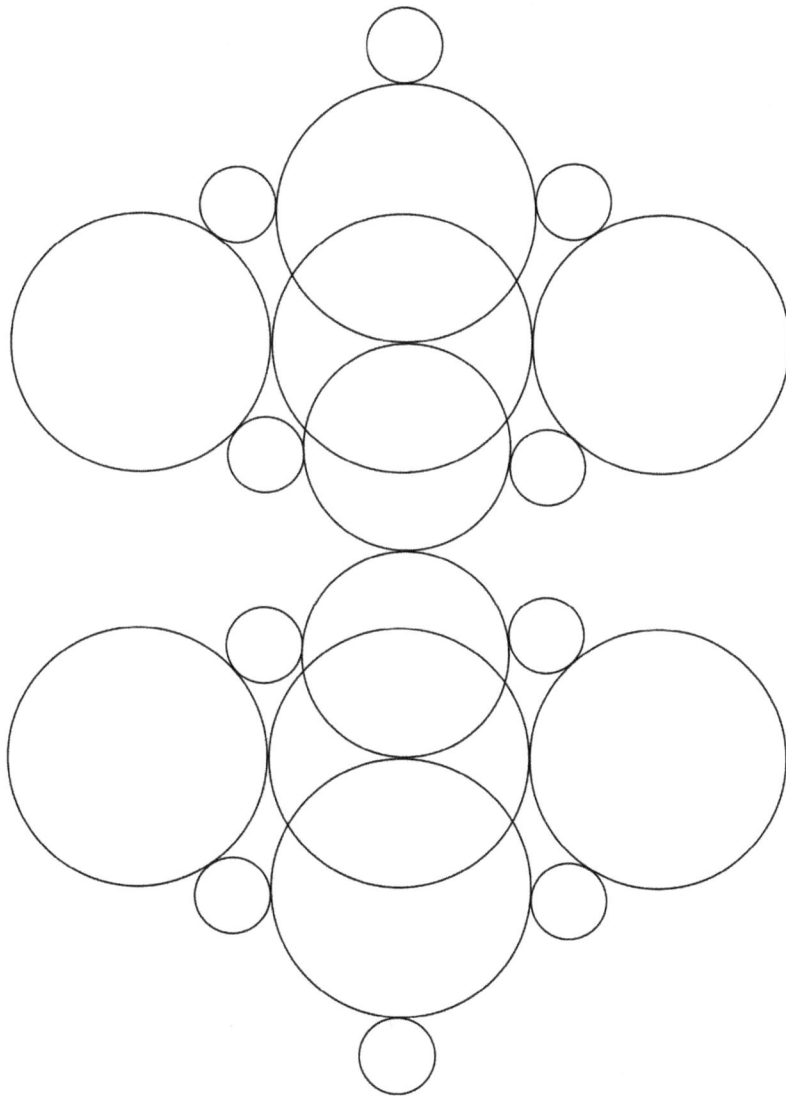

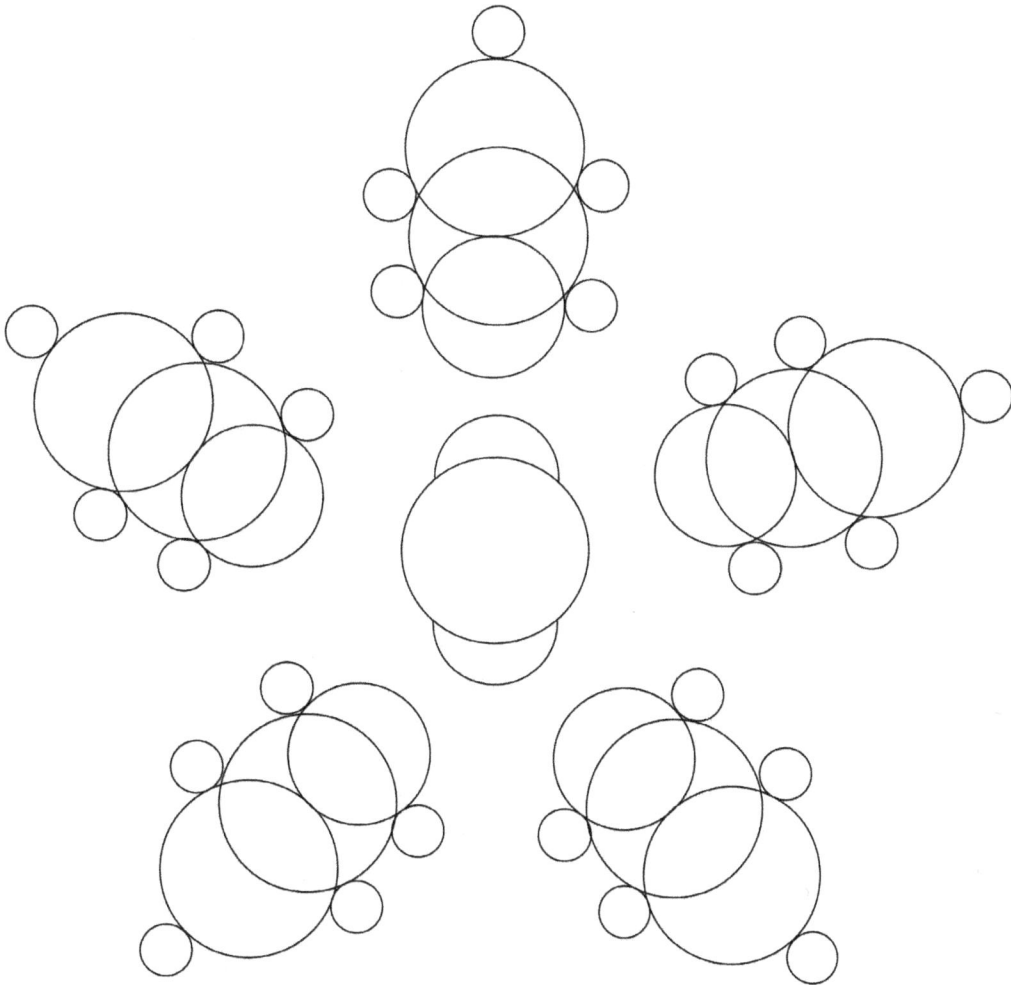

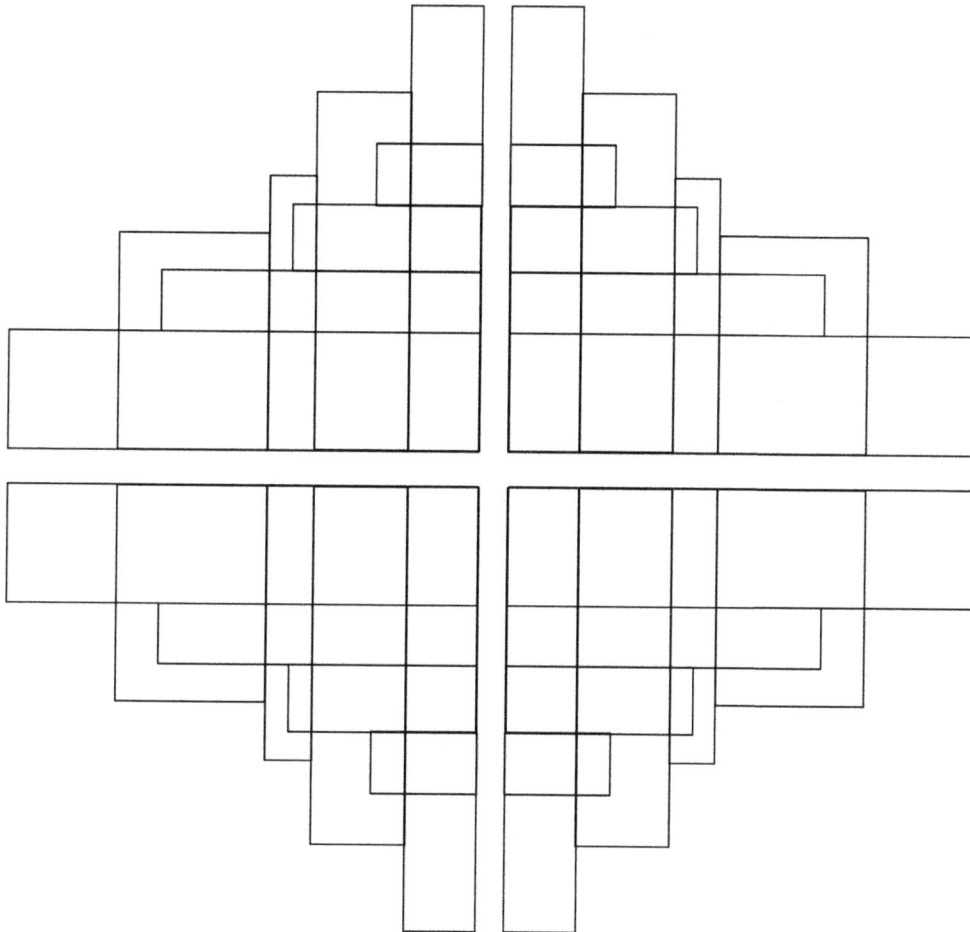

Reference Graph 34A

Reference Graph 34B

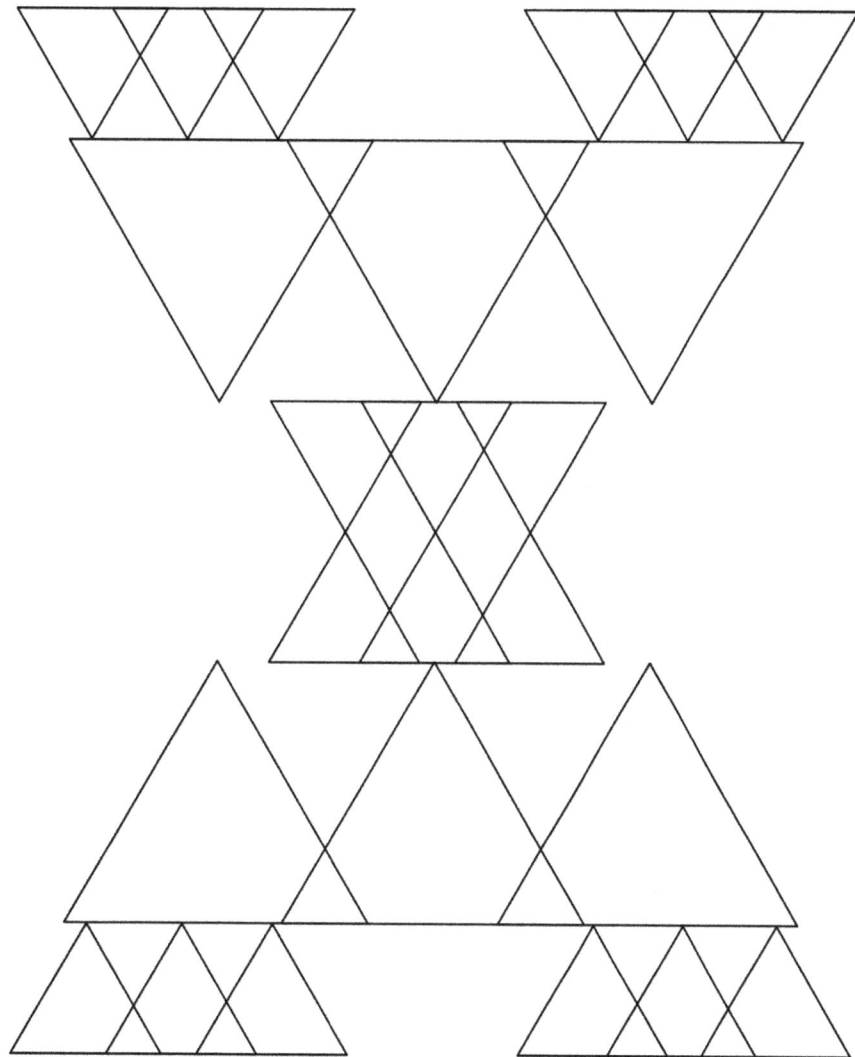

Reference Graph 36B

Reference Graph 38A

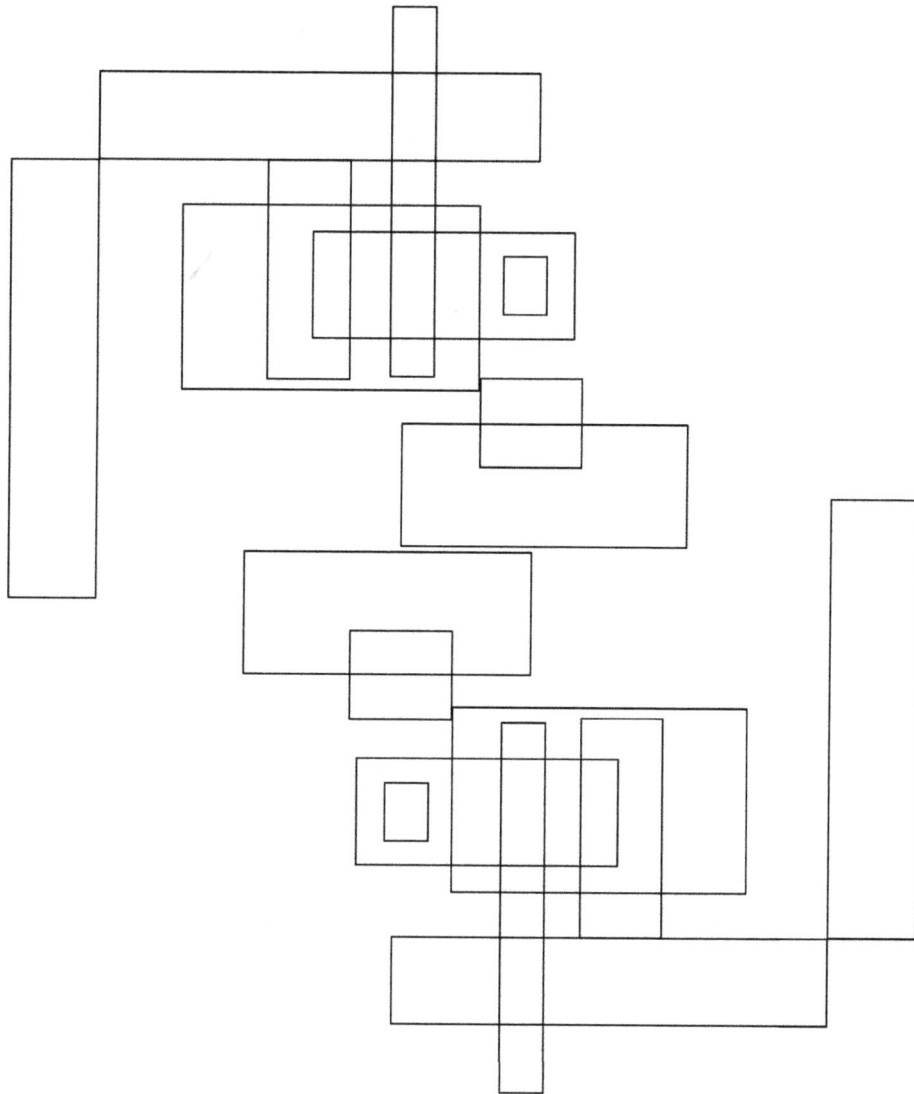

157

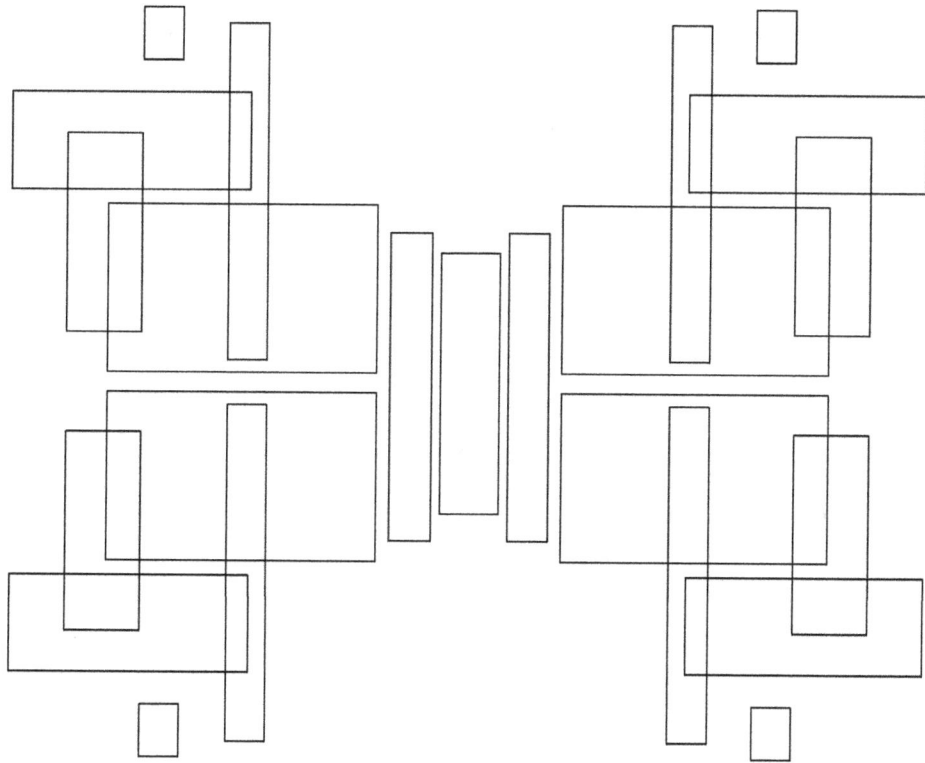

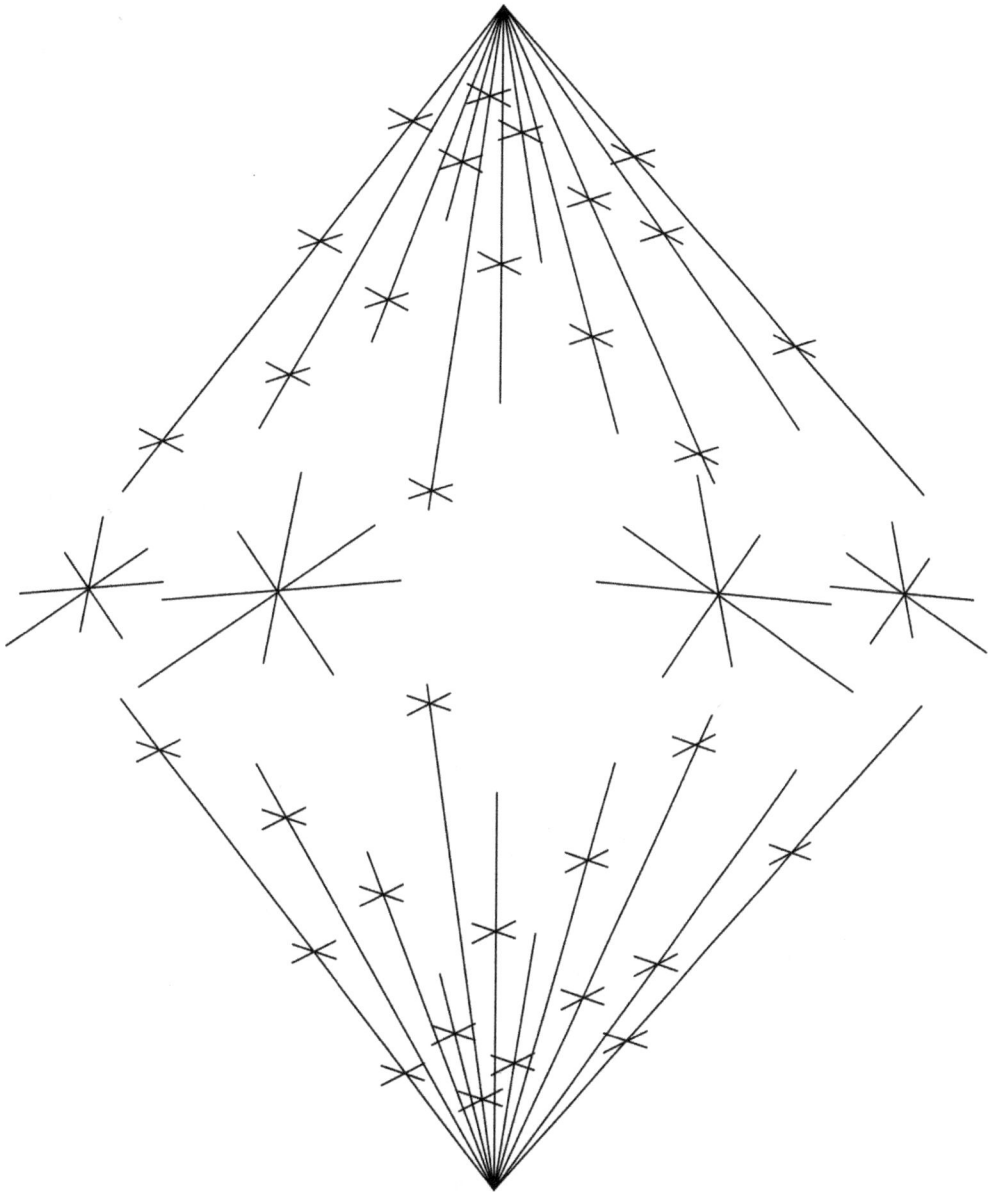

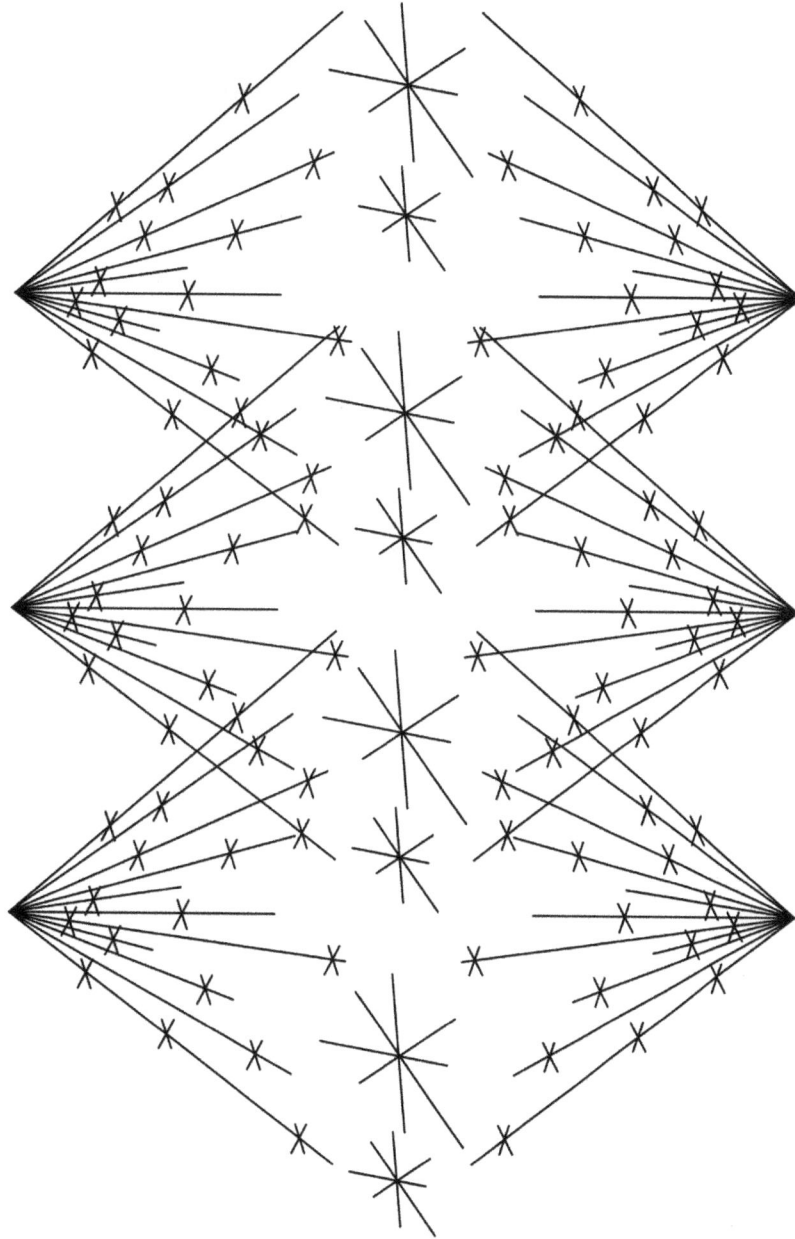

Reference Graph 40A

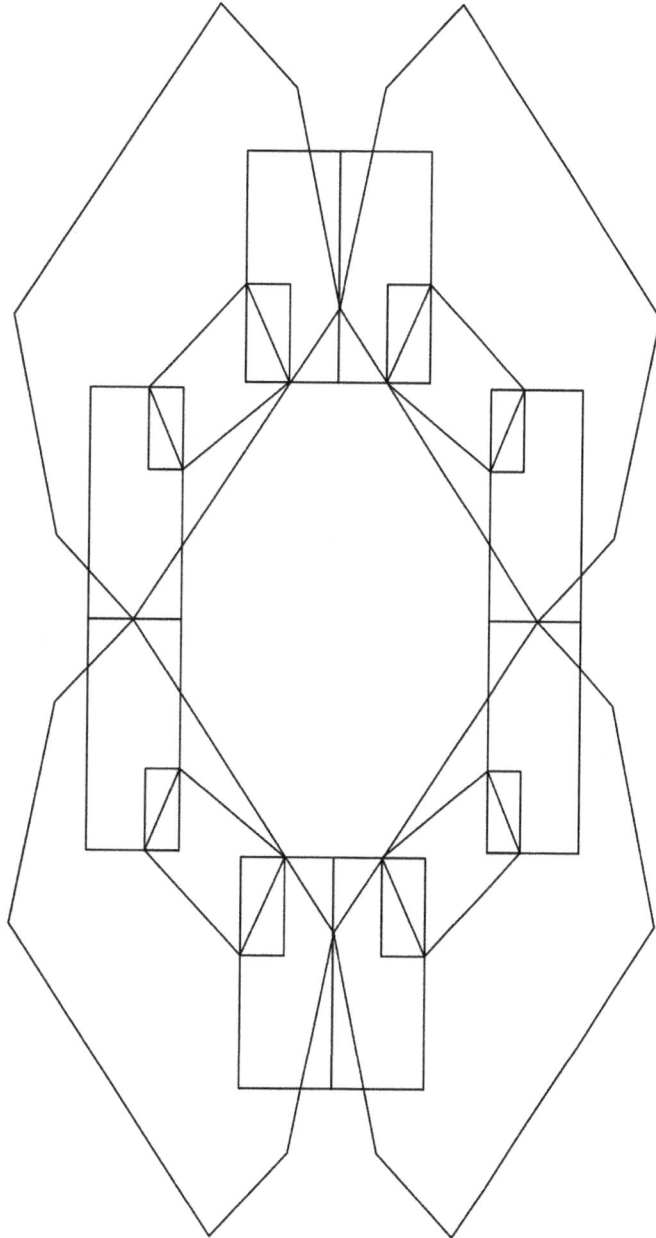

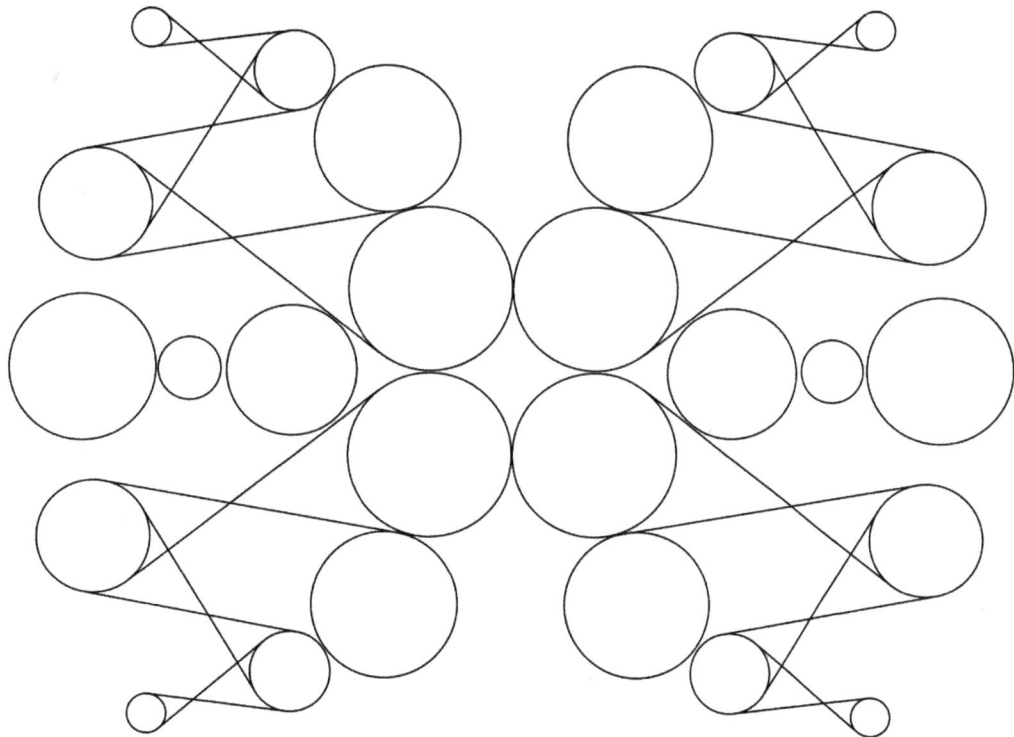

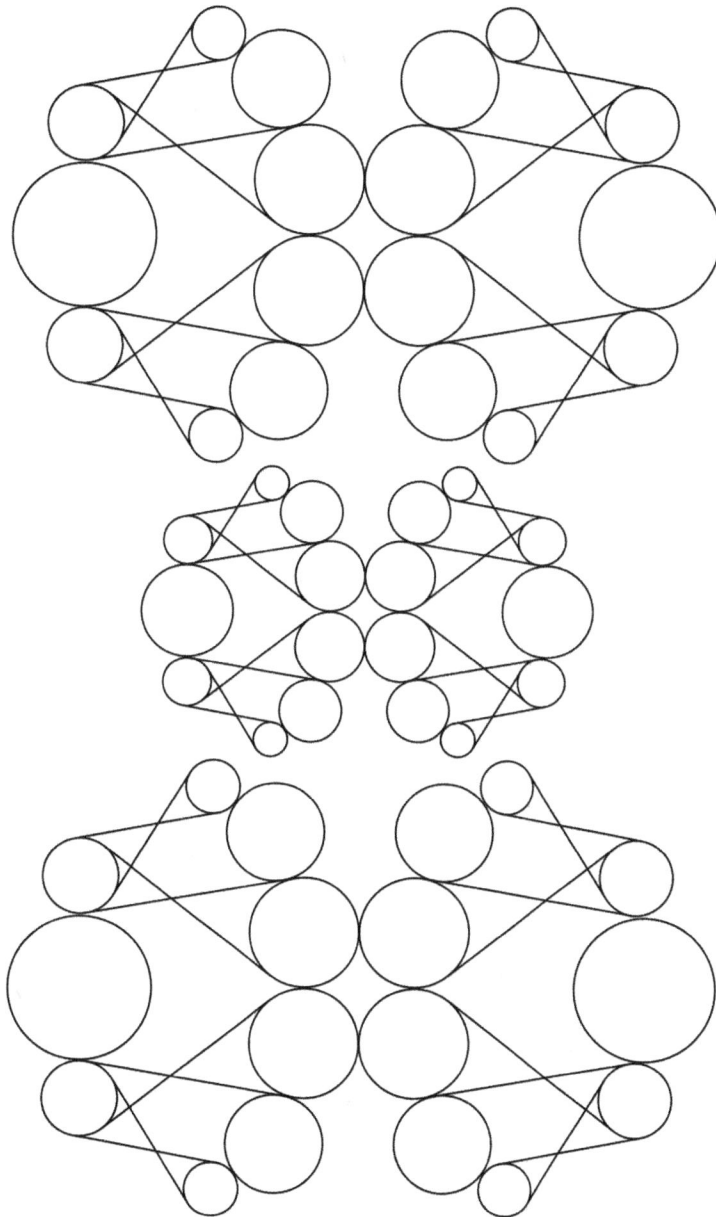

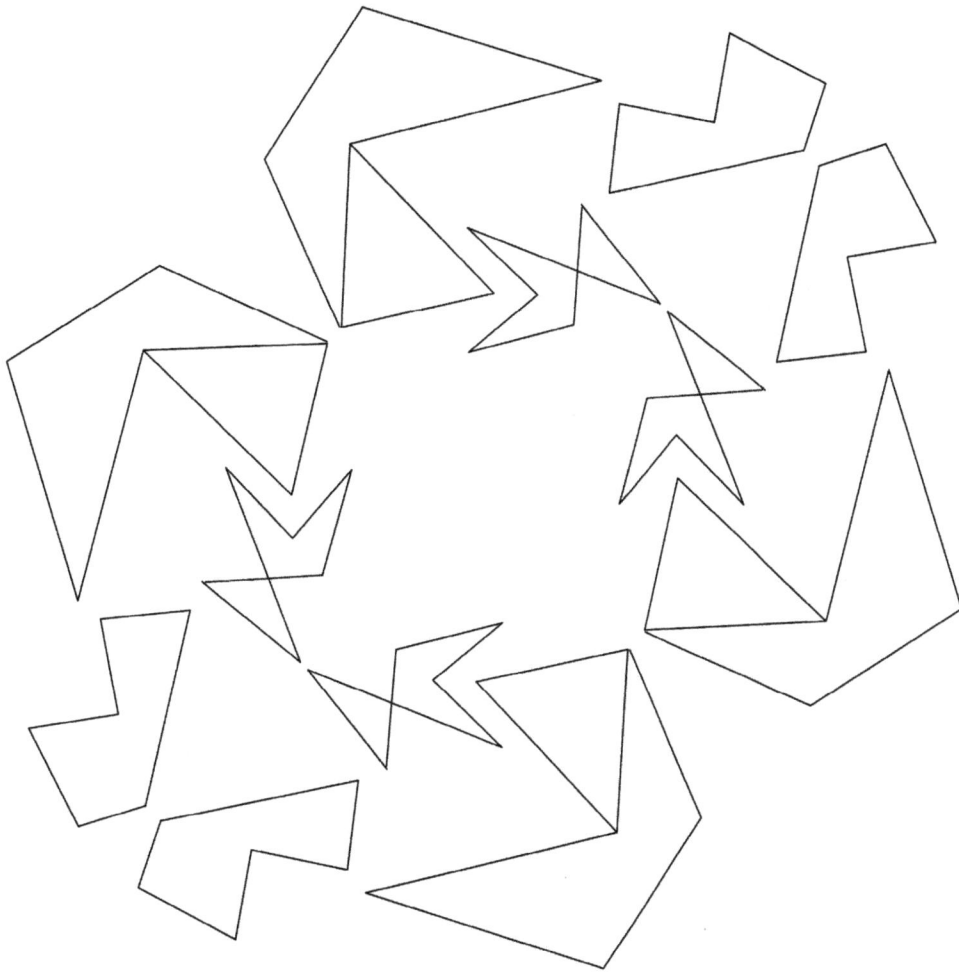

Reference Graph 44B

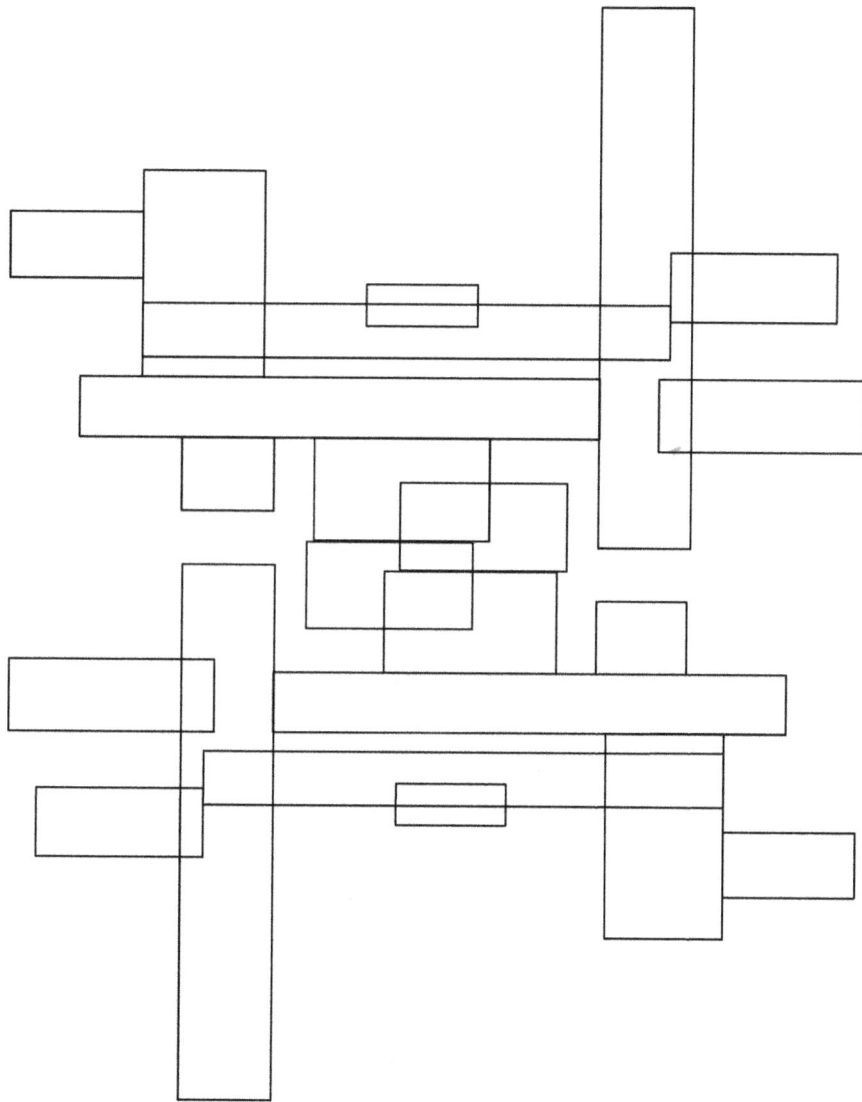

183